EXTRAORDINARY
Latinas

VOLUME IV
FEARLESS NARRATIVES
OF TRIUMPH, UNITY & PURPOSE

PRESENTED BY
ILHIANA ROJAS SALDANA &
SANDRA NOEMI TORRES

EXTRAORDINARY LATINAS VOL IV
FEARLESS NARRATIVES OF TRIUMPH, UNITY & PURPOSE

Published by:
Ilhiana Rojas Saldana
& Sandra Noemi Torres
www.unitedlatinas.com

Editing by Lora Denton
Masters in Clarity | www.mastersinclarity.com

ISBN: 979-8-9925568-0-3

Published in the United States of America

To the extraordinary Latinas who rise every day, carrying dreams that go beyond their own. Your strength, courage, and love inspire generations. May you always remember that your story matters and your dreams are worth pursuing—just as someone once quietly reminded me.

Ilhiana

It's not about being fearless, it's about learning to experience fear less.
Trusting that the world you desire to create is waiting for you to create it.

I have learned that nothing is impossible when you believe that you are worthy
of creating the life you want.

Triumph is possible when you boldly take the steps needed to get yourself where you want
to go. Doing something despite uncertainties is the bravest thing one can do.

Finding unity with others and realizing sometimes we aren't meant to do things alone is a
key to your success. Form partnerships, alliances and support others and in return the
universe will gift that back to you.

Understanding your purpose in this life is a blessing. Find Life's meaning or simply give
it meaning. You are responsible for this. You are designed for this.
And you are the one in control of this.

To all the women who contributed to this book, thank you for your words &
vulnerability, thank you for your work and thank you for being part of our United
Latinas community.

Sandra Noemi

TABLE OF CONTENTS

ACKNOWLEDGEMENTS

We extend our deepest gratitude to everyone whose dedication and hard work made this book possible. A special thanks to our extraordinary co-authors, who generously shared their stories and wisdom, embodying the remarkable leaders they have become. Your belief in this project and trust throughout the journey have been invaluable.

Our heartfelt appreciation goes to Lora Denton and the Masters in Clarity team (www.mastersinclarity.com) for their unwavering behind-the-scenes support, which has been instrumental in bringing this book to life.

A sincere thank you to the incredible members of UNITED LATINAS. Your commitment, passion, and engagement have been essential in creating a thriving community that continues to inspire and uplift Extraordinary Latinas everywhere.

At UNITED LATINAS, we firmly believe that we rise by lifting others. We are sincerely grateful to all who have chosen to walk this path with us, contributing to this shared vision of empowerment and growth.

Ilhiana & Sandra

MightyHUB

Power Up Your Network and Become a part of the UL Online Community

unitedlatinas.mn.co

LATINAS ARE A FORCE OF NATURE

FOREWORD BY:

CYNTHIA KLEINBAUM MILNER

When I asked to write this foreword, I felt an electric sense of purpose. This book, *Extraordinary Latinas Vol IV*, is more than a collection of stories—it's a movement. It's a blueprint for transformation, a rallying cry for greatness, and a reminder that the extraordinary potential within each of us can—and must—be unleashed.

Let's start with the truth: Latinas are a force of nature. We're not just contributors to the world—we are creators. We bring a unique blend of passion, resilience, and determination to everything we do. Yet, for too long, the world has failed to recognize our power. It's time to change that. It's time to flip the script and embrace the truth that being Latina isn't just a part of who we are—it's our superpower.

Latinas are the backbone of America's cultural and economic engine. We are the fastest-growing demographic in the U.S., control an increasing share of household purchasing power, and earn more degrees than ever before. Yet, despite all of this, the representation of Latinas in leadership remains abysmally low. It's not just unfair; it's bad business. Companies, communities, and countries thrive when leadership reflects the diversity of the people it serves. And right now, we're leaving value—massive value—on the table by failing to elevate Latinas.

This book, *Extraordinary Latinas Vol IV*, is part manifesto, part strategy guide, and part call to arms. It's about flipping the script—not just for Latinas, but for everyone who benefits when we unlock the potential of an overlooked and underestimated force.

This book is about more than representation. It's about *transformation*. It's about moving from surviving to thriving, from being underestimated to being unstoppable. The women featured in these pages prove that anything is possible when you step into your power, own your story, and refuse to be limited by anyone else's expectations.

But success doesn't happen by accident. It happens by design. You need a vision. You need a strategy. And you need the courage to take bold, massive action. That's what these stories provide—a roadmap for creating a life and career that's not just successful but meaningful, fulfilling, and aligned with who you truly are.

One of the most powerful lessons in this book is the importance of reframing what it means to be Latina. Think about it: How often have you been told to "tone it down"? Is your loudness, your accent, or your passion a problem? Let me tell you something—those are your gifts. Your loudness? That's energy that moves people to action. Your accent? That's a testament to your ability to navigate multiple worlds, bringing unique insights and perspectives to the table. Your passion? That's the fire that inspires and fuels greatness.

When you embrace these qualities instead of suppressing them, you unlock an unstoppable level of power. And that's what the women in this book have done. They've learned to own their authentic selves and use their unique qualities to lead, inspire, and create impact.

Success is a team sport. No one gets to the top on their own. That's why this book is so important—it's not just a collection of stories; it's a community. It's a reminder that a network of Latinas are cheering for you, rooting for you, and ready to lift you up.

But here's the deal: inspiration isn't enough. You've got to take action. You've got to set big, bold goals and commit to them with everything you've got. You must surround yourself with people who push you to grow, challenge you to be better, and hold you accountable to your highest potential.

The women featured in *Extraordinary Latinas Vol IV* are living proof that success isn't about conforming to someone else's definition of leadership. It's about redefining leadership to be true to who you are. They've fought battles—external and internal—and emerged stronger, wiser, and more impactful. These stories aren't just inspiring; they're actionable. They show what's possible when you embrace your authenticity and use it as a lever for success.

To the Latinas reading this: You already have everything you need to succeed. The only thing standing between you and your dreams is the story you tell yourself. Are you telling yourself that you're not enough? That the odds are stacked against you? Stop. Right now. Flip that story. Tell yourself the truth: You are powerful beyond measure. You are capable of extraordinary things. And you are not alone.

And most importantly, you've got to believe in yourself. Not just in your skills or talent but in your ability to create change—to rewrite the rules, lead authentically, and build a life that reflects your deepest values and highest aspirations.

This book is your playbook. Use it. Let it inspire you, but don't stop there. Take the lessons, the strategies, and the stories and put them into action. Because the world needs what only you can bring.

To the extraordinary women featured in this book: *Thank you for your courage, vulnerability, and leadership. You are paving the way for a brighter, more inclusive future.*

To the next generation of Latinas: *Your time is now. Step into your power. Embrace your superpowers. And remember, success isn't about doing it alone—it's about lifting as you climb and creating a ripple effect that transforms the world.*

So, let's go. Let's flip the script. Let's show the world what's possible when Latinas lead. And let's create a legacy that will inspire generations to come.

With energy, passion, and belief in your greatness,

Cynthia Kleinbaum Milner
Co-founder and President, A LA LATINA

~ ~ ~

Cynthia Kleinbaum is a global marketing leader and the co-creator of *A LA LATINA: The Playbook To Succeed Being Your Authentic Self*, a multimedia platform designed to support Latinas at all career levels in reaching the top of Corporate America. With over 20 years of experience, she has built a reputation for reimagining customer engagement strategies to accelerate business growth. Most recently, she served as the Chief Marketing Officer at MoneyLion (NYSE: ML), leading marketing efforts to drive customer acquisition and brand expansion. Prior to that, she held multiple leadership roles at Walmart (NYSE: WMT), including Vice President of Marketing for Walmart+, Mobile Apps, and Online Grocery, where she played a key role in strengthening Walmart's omnichannel competitive positioning.

Throughout her career, Cynthia has leveraged her expertise in both brand and performance marketing to transform businesses ranging from startups to global enterprises. She successfully repositioned Bonobos by emphasizing its inclusive design and modernizing its customer acquisition strategy, launched Gilt Groupe's loyalty program and first physical retail store to enhance customer retention, and revitalized the Nesquik brand in Mexico to embrace its fun and playful identity. Earlier in her career, she contributed to strategic initiatives as a consultant at The Boston Consulting Group. A Harvard Business School MBA graduate with a B.A. from Universidad Iberoamericana in Mexico City, Cynthia is a sought-after speaker at industry conferences, sharing insights on high-performing marketing organizations, startup innovation within corporations, and data-driven marketing strategies. She has been recognized as a CSA Top Woman in Tech (2020), a Brand

Innovators Woman to Watch (2021), and a 2023 International Women's Fellow.

~ ~ ~

Connect with Cynthia:
https://www.linkedin.com/in/cynthia-kleinbaum-milner-63685b2/

INTRODUCTION BY:

ILHIANA ROJAS SALDANA

What's your story?

It's a question that carries a profound weight. Our stories shape us—our hopes, our fears, our triumphs, and the journeys that have brought us to this moment. For so long, I never truly reflected on my own story. I didn't understand the transformative power of owning it. I didn't realize that sharing my truth—and hearing the truths of others— could become a powerful force of healing, empowerment, and inspiration.

But life has a way of teaching us when we are ready to listen.

Until recently, I started to think about my mother's story—an extraordinary story of grit, resilience, and passion. She was unstoppable. At just 15 years old, growing up in Mexico in the 1960s, she made a bold declaration: she would visit every country in the world. For many, that would have remained just a dream, especially for a young woman navigating the challenges and societal expectations of that time. But not my mother. Nothing could stop her. She found ways to overcome every obstacle one by one.

When she met my father, she told him plainly that if he wanted to marry her, he would have to join her in this dream of seeing the world. And together, they made it happen. Even after my brother and I were born, she never let motherhood become an excuse to give up her dreams. If anything, motherhood inspired her to push even further.

She decided to go back to college, earning a degree in International Relations and later a Master's. I have vivid memories of those years—going to school in the mornings and then accompanying her to her college classes in the afternoons and evenings. I would sit quietly at the back of the classroom, watching her pursue her education with relentless passion.

But that wasn't all. My mother's passion for learning and for the arts shaped the next chapter of her life. She became a renowned sculptor and painter, using her knowledge of international relations to promote art and culture across borders. She uplifted not just herself but countless others along the way.

Even now, in her passing, as I go through her belongings, I continue to learn more about her – pieces of her journey I never knew that I wish I could sit down and hear from her directly. With each new discovery, she has become even more extraordinary to me, and her story deepens my commitment to this mission: elevating and honoring the narratives of others.

This commitment is what drives the Extraordinary Latinas series. In this fourth volume we celebrate 18 fearless stories of triumph, unity and purpose. Each story is unique, yet they all share the same spirit of resilience and strength that I admire so deeply in my mother. These women have faced obstacles, self-doubt, and systemic challenges, yet they persevered with a powerful sense of purpose. They embody what it means to be extraordinary.

As Latinas, we come from a lineage of powerful women—our madres, abuelas, tias—who often carried the weight of the world on their shoulders without complaint. Their sacrifices, triumphs, and unyielding hope are woven into the fabric of who we are. They taught us that no challenge is insurmountable and that the power of unity and community can propel us forward.

Yet, for many of us, there comes a moment when we lose sight of that power. I lived that moment during the last part of my corporate life. I had a successful career at Fortune 500 companies, climbing the ladder and achieving the kind of accolades many dream of. But despite that success, there was a point where I felt lost—empty, full of fear and self-doubt. Without realizing it, I had assimilated into a culture that wasn't my own, and in the process, I lost connection with who I truly was. I didn't fit in, and that isolation left me broken inside.

It wasn't until I heard the stories of other remarkable Latinas—stories of courage, vulnerability, and triumph—that I found the strength to reclaim my power. Their stories reminded me that I wasn't alone. They became a mirror, reflecting the possibility of a new life that I could envision and create for myself. Their journeys fueled my belief that I could rise again.

Today, the success I hold as a serial entrepreneur is built on that foundation of shared wisdom and inspiration. This is why I am so passionate about this series—because I know firsthand the life-changing impact of hearing someone else's truth. I want every reader to feel that same empowerment and connection

Sharing our stories is not just about personal healing; it is an act of empowerment and legacy. When we own and share our narratives, we inspire others to do the same. We create a ripple effect that strengthens our communities and uplifts future generations. Our stories are a light and a fuel, igniting hope and courage in the hearts of those who walk beside us and those who come after us.

To you, I say this: Embrace your story. Honor every part of your journey— the triumphs and the struggles. Know that you are part of a powerful legacy, and your voice matters. Let the stories in this book inspire you to believe in your own potential. Let them remind you of the strength, unity, and purpose that run through your veins.

And when you are ready, I hope you'll envision yourself as a future author in the *Extraordinary Latinas* series. We need your voice. The world needs your voice.

You were born to be extraordinary. Now is the time to reclaim your power and let your light shine.

The world is waiting.

In gratitude,

Ilhiana

~ ~ ~

Ilhiana Rojas is a seasoned Business Strategist, Executive and Leadership Transformational Coach, a Diversity & Inclusion Consultant, an Award-winning Advocate for women and Hispanics, a multiple Bestselling Author, and an International Motivational Speaker. She is a possibility thinker and a firm believer that nothing is impossible. Ilhiana uses her 20-plus years of corporate experience and certified coaching expertise to help build resilient, collaborative, and high-performing leaders and cultures. Ilhiana also serves on multiple Boards supporting initiatives that center on empowering women and Hispanic populations.

~ ~ ~

Connect with Ilhiana
https://www.linkedin.com/in/ilhiana-rojas7
www.belivecoach.com
www.unitedlatinas.com
Email: ilhiana@unitedlatinas.com

ANNIE REYES

"I am committed to empowering a lasting legacy of art, community, and well-being, ensuring it continues to inspire and uplift at any age or circumstance of life for years to come."

\-   Annie Reyes

~ ~ ~

Annie Reyes, a dynamic Latina businesswoman with Cuban and Venezuelan roots, has built a remarkable career grounded in creativity, resilience, and a deep commitment to community. After early recognition in Venezuela, where she won the "Mara de Oro" award for Marketing Woman of the Year, she relocated to Miami due to political unrest. Overcoming language barriers and self-doubt, she became the Promotions Director for the Kiwanis Club of Little Havana, managing major events like the Calle Ocho Music Festival.

In her late 50s, Annie achieved these remarkable milestones, including founding Hivedeco in 2020, where she merged art and well-being by creating over 500 commissioned art pieces and publishing coloring books to promote mental health. In 2024, she earned an Art Therapy Certification, was named Florida's Best Coloring Book Author, and was nominated for the Connecting Community Award by United Latinas Inc. Most recently, Annie was honored as the winner of the 2024 Female Voice Awards in the Inner Peace Category by WomELLE, showing that it's never too late to pursue your dreams.

~ ~ ~

In memory of my wonderful parents, and with deep gratitude to my daughter Stefania, my son Juan Carlos, my sisters, and my nephews, who have been my pillars of strength. To my granddaughters Valentina and Victoria, whose joy lights up my heart, and to my husband Andres, whose unwavering support makes this journey possible. This book is a tribute to the love, resilience, and unity that bind us all.

THE TRANSFORMATIVE POWER OF ART

THE JOURNEY

My journey is deeply rooted in a rich cultural heritage shaped by my Cuban and Venezuelan roots. Growing up in Venezuela, my Cuban family instilled in me the values of hard work, determination, and the belief that education was the key to success. These principles formed the foundation of my work ethic, driving me to excel in all my endeavors.

My journey has also been shaped by an early fascination with art, which blossomed as I painted the bulletin boards at the Catholic school I attended. I still remember sitting with the nuns, who would bring cookies and sodas, chatting with me while I worked on my paintings. I also have fond memories of accompanying my mother to her art classes. She painted on porcelain, and to this day, I vividly recall how she mixed the colors—I can even smell the paints. It's funny because when I think about it, the memories play out in slow motion in my mind.

I got married young, at just 17, and a couple of years later, my first son, Juan Carlos, was born. I began studying graphic design—it was the closest I could get to art while still being able to care for my little one. A few years later, my beautiful daughter, Stefania, was born.

Sometime later, after my divorce and now a single mother of two, life led me to work in marketing for the music industry. I was pretty successful, even winning a prestigious national award in Venezuela called "El Mara de Oro" for Best Marketing Executive.

Despite my professional success, Venezuela's political and security issues forced me to make the difficult decision to emigrate to this beautiful country, accompanied by my two children.

Arriving in this country with two children without knowing the language was a huge challenge. Not only was it difficult to find work, but even helping my kids with their schoolwork was frustrating because sometimes I didn't understand what it was about. I juggled various jobs initially—working in sales, as a waitress, and doing freelance graphic design work.

Then 9/11 happened. The entire country felt an overwhelming sadness for what had occurred. The heaviness in the air was palpable everywhere. It was then that I decided, in the face of so much destruction, that I needed to create.

Two days later, I went out and bought a sheet of Sheetrock and started painting. That's when my first mural was born. The experience filled me with a deep sense of purpose, and I enrolled in a short mural art course at Miami-Dade College. Soon after, I started receiving mural commissions.

While juggling several jobs like a performer spinning plates, I finally bought my son a car in his last year of high school, allowing him to get a job at Blockbuster. After graduation, he decided to move to Orlando for college, leaving me in Miami with my daughter Stefania. Today, my children are wonderful human beings, and my daughter has made me a proud grandmother to two princesses, Valentina and Victoria.

In 2010, my sister and I founded a marketing agency, again setting aside my true passion—art. Those were years of great learning and growth. I also began working with the Kiwanis Club of Little Havana as an independent contractor that same year. This opportunity allowed me to apply my marketing skills while deepening my commitment to community engagement. By 2019, I was promoted to Promotions Director, responsible for marketing the organization's various community projects, including free summer camps, one of the nation's largest Back to School programs, and the renowned Calle Ocho Music Festival—the most prominent Latin festival in the U.S.

Being a Latina businesswoman in the U.S. came with its challenges. The language barrier often triggered feelings of inadequacy, leading to what many know as "impostor syndrome." Despite my professional experience, I questioned my abilities and whether I deserved the opportunities that came my way.

Then COVID-19 hit in 2020. It was another painful event, but it reignited my artistic vein. While stuck at home, I decided to start painting cheeseboards. What began as a small project turned into a great success. I received over 500 commissions for custom-made, hand-painted cheeseboards in two years.

During the pandemic, I found solace through my faith in God and through art. This challenging period made me realize how much art can help overcome difficult times, and I wanted others to experience the same sense of peace.

In 2021, in my mid-50s, while continuing my role with Kiwanis, I founded Hivedeco. Balancing two demanding roles often meant working more than 14 hours daily, but my passion drove me. Hivedeco became an outlet for my creativity, allowing me to channel my love for art into creating adult coloring books. These books serve as stress relief and creativity tools, helping individuals explore their artistic skills and find peace in the process.

Within less than a year, I published ten coloring books, now available on over 15 major online platforms, including Amazon, Barnes & Noble, and Walmart. The response has been overwhelming, with countless testimonials from individuals and mental health institutions praising the positive impact of my books on those dealing with depression and anxiety.

Each challenge along this journey taught me valuable lessons about resilience, adaptability, and staying true to my passions. I realized that my experiences were not just about building a career but about creating a legacy rooted in community, creativity, and empowerment.

Creating art is profound, and I wanted others to experience that joy—not just by admiring art but by creating something beautiful themselves. This desire led to the founding of Hivedeco, which, despite the demands of my role at Kiwanis, became a thriving venture promoting relaxation and well-being through art.

Through Hivedeco, I aimed to empower individuals to engage in the creative process, fostering a sense of community and accomplishment. Creating and sharing art builds bridges between people, creating spaces where joy, fulfillment, and connection thrive.

In 2024, I achieved a significant milestone by earning my Certification in Art Therapy, underscoring my commitment to using art for relaxation and well-being. That same year, I was honored with the Best Coloring Book Author in Florida award by Best of Best Review. My efforts to foster community and support others were further recognized with a nomination for the Connecting Community Award by United Latinas and as the winner of the 2024 Female Voice Awards in the Inner Peace Category by WomELLE, highlighting the impact of using art to bring people together and create positive change.

I have always believed in the transformative power of art. My work is driven by a deep commitment to promoting mental health and well-being through creative expression. Whether through in-person events or the pages of my coloring books, my goal is to provide people with the opportunity to experience the joy of creativity, the satisfaction of accomplishment, and the sense of belonging that comes from being part of a community united by a shared love of art.

THE LEARNINGS

I've encountered numerous challenges that have profoundly shaped who I am today. Moving to the United States as a single mother brought significant obstacles, including learning a new language and adapting to a completely different culture.

However, my faith in God has always been my secure foundation, providing guidance and strength during difficult times. My family and a few close friends have been an unwavering support system. As a close-knit Hispanic family, we celebrate each other's successes with genuine joy, and their belief in me helped me push through moments of doubt and fear.

In addition to my deep faith in God and the belief that He always guides our steps, I have realized that there is no greater achievement than one that is shared. We all possess a gift, and once we discover and develop it, the greatest satisfaction comes when we use it to help others. I've learned that we must combat destruction with creation when we encounter destruction. I've also understood that we each have a mission, and while our free will may lead us down different paths, life always brings us back to the beautiful road designed for us.

> *We all possess a gift, and once we discover and develop it, the greatest satisfaction comes when we use it to help others.*

Deep in my heart, I know my purpose is to help others through art. I began by assisting the nuns at my school with painting bulletin boards, creating murals and utilitarian pieces that brought joy to homes, designing graphics for various industries that helped them increase their sales, and working with non-profit organizations to support their missions in assisting communities.

My coloring book illustrations have touched the lives of hundreds, helping people relax, feel a sense of accomplishment, and find a connection within a larger community. Although I've strayed from this path sometimes, I've always found my way back.

It doesn't matter where you were born or what language you speak; if a significant part of your life is dedicated to improving the lives of others, you are a universal being, and your words will always be understood through the hearts of others.

One of the most pivotal lessons I've learned is the importance of re-evaluating situations to find a more positive understanding of the factors at play. This shift in perspective allowed me to see age not as a disadvantage but a tremendous asset. With age comes experience, wisdom, and a deeper understanding of life's complexities. I realized that these qualities could empower me to achieve my goals and, more importantly, to help others along the way.

Founding Hivedeco in my mid-50s was a turning point. I began to see my creative work not just as a personal achievement but as a contribution to the well-being of others. The testimonials from people who have benefited from my coloring books, especially those dealing with mental health challenges like depression and anxiety, have been incredibly rewarding. Knowing that my work has brought joy, peace, and a sense of community to others has given me a profound sense of purpose.

Coping with language, age, and impostor syndrome challenges required me to reassess and redefine my approach to these obstacles constantly. By reframing my thoughts, I discovered that my dreams could fulfill my personal aspirations and lead to a better life for others. This understanding has been incredibly motivating and has driven me to focus my work on bringing happiness and wellness to others through art.

Ultimately, my challenges have taught me the importance of perseverance, faith, and the power of a positive mindset. My journey has shown me that when we align our dreams with a commitment to improving the lives of others, we can overcome any obstacle. Age, language, and self-doubt become stepping stones rather than barriers, leading to a life filled with purpose, joy, and connection.

THE INSPIRATION

God has been my most significant source of inspiration and strength throughout my life. My parents, who arrived in Venezuela from Cuba, instilled in me the importance of hard work, resilience, and education. Their example of starting over in a new country with determination and hope has always inspired me to push forward despite challenges.

Moving to the United States as a single mother, learning a new language, and starting over in a completely different environment were some of the most challenging experiences of my life. However, the values my parents instilled in me helped me persevere, reminding me that it's never too late to rebuild, learn, and grow.

The COVID-19 pandemic was a particularly trying time for many, including myself. During this period of uncertainty and isolation, I rediscovered my passion for art, realizing it could bring healing and joy to myself and others. This marked a turning point, inspiring me to channel my creativity into something meaningful.

I have always believed in the power of art to transform lives and build stronger communities. My work is driven by a deep commitment to promoting mental health and well-being through creative expression.

Engaging with various communities, I've seen firsthand the positive impact that art can have on individuals dealing with anxiety, stress, and other challenges. One of the most rewarding aspects of my work has been organizing events where participants can experience the uplifting effects of coloring. These events provide a space for people to come together, relax, and connect through the simple act of coloring. The feedback has been overwhelmingly positive, with many participants sharing how coloring has helped them manage anxiety, find moments of peace, and feel a deeper connection to a community. I have received countless testimonials from followers who have purchased my books, expressing how these coloring books have been instrumental in helping them cope with depression and anxiety. Knowing that my work makes a difference in people's lives is incredibly fulfilling.

I have a client in Dallas, Texas, who is a therapist at a mental health facility. She purchased several of my coloring books for her therapy sessions with patients. She was amazed at the level of relaxation her patients experienced, and some of them even asked to buy the books directly from me.

In another event, I had a group of women coloring at a table, and one of them shared that she had just gone through a challenging situation at home. She initially said relaxing would be impossible because she was so upset— she couldn't stop talking. But just a few minutes later, there was absolute silence. Without even realizing it, her mind had calmed down.

Another moment that left a mark on me happened during an event where a senior woman was sitting at a table. Everyone around her was coloring one of my books, but she wasn't given one. When I asked about it, they told me she had Alzheimer's and didn't engage much. But I noticed she was watching everyone and seemed to feel left out. So, I approached her and placed an illustration and some crayons in front of her. She smiled at me and started to color. I cried.

Artists like Frida Kahlo have long inspired me, particularly in how she transformed personal pain into influential, transformative art. Her ability to convey deep emotion through her work resonated with me, especially as I faced challenges. Over time, my inspiration evolved from simply admiring art to using creativity to promote wellness and build a sense of community. I began creating coloring books for adults, using art to help others find relaxation and peace in a world filled with stress and anxiety.

Creativity is not just about making something beautiful; it's about finding strength, expressing emotions, and connecting with others on a deeper level.

Today, I am driven by the desire to inspire others, especially women, to embrace their creativity and overcome life's challenges—whether starting over in a new country, learning a new language, dealing with anxiety, or facing the doubts that come with age. My journey has taught me that creativity is not just about making something beautiful; it's about finding strength, expressing emotions, and connecting with others on a deeper level.

Through my work, I aim to create a space where people can explore their creativity, find comfort in their faith, and build a supportive community. Art has the power to heal, bring people together, and inspire positive change. By sharing my story and art, I hope to encourage others to pursue their passions, regardless of age or circumstances, and find the same sense of fulfillment and joy I have discovered through creativity and faith.

Ultimately, it's about more than just creating art; it's about creating a legacy of resilience, hope, and connection. We can overcome the most daunting challenges with faith, perseverance, and creativity and find beauty in the journey.

THE ADVICE

If I could advise my younger self, it would be to embrace every part of your journey, including the challenges, with confidence and grace. I would remind myself that every obstacle, whether a language barrier, the doubts that come with age, or the feelings of inadequacy and impostor syndrome, is not just a hurdle but a stepping stone to growth. I wish I had realized earlier that I am not defined by the limitations others might perceive but by the strength, creativity, and compassion I bring to the world.

A fundamental shift in mindset that I wish I had adopted sooner is understanding that success is not just about personal achievement. True fulfillment comes from using our talents to lift others as we climb. We begin to see the profound impact we can have when we harness our gifts, not just for our growth but to support and empower others. Embracing our culture, loving others as we love ourselves, and nurturing our creativity are universal languages. Through these, we can open doors that once seemed closed and find common ground with people from all walks of life.

To anyone going through a similar journey, never underestimate the power of your voice, talents, and heritage.

The journey might be challenging, especially when you are faced with starting over in a new country, learning a new language, or stepping into a new phase of life. But remember, you are a complete human being, beautifully crafted with unique gifts meant to be shared with the world.

Daily reflection through journaling is one of the habits that has been instrumental in my personal growth. This practice helps me to re-evaluate situations, allowing me to find a more positive understanding of the factors at play and the lessons that can be learned from past experiences.

Another essential habit is continuous learning. Whether through books, courses or simply staying curious, I've learned that growth doesn't stop at a certain age or level of achievement; it's a lifelong journey.

Gratitude is another powerful practice that has shaped my perspective. Taking time each day to acknowledge the blessings in my life, even in difficult times, has helped me stay grounded and focused on what truly matters. It's a reminder that every step of the journey, even the challenging ones, is part of a larger picture of growth and purpose.

Lastly, embracing creativity in all forms has been a cornerstone of my personal and professional life. Whether through art, writing, or problem-solving, creativity allows us to see the world through a lens of possibility rather than limitation. It's a tool that not only enriches our own lives but can be used to inspire and uplift those around us.

Ultimately, my advice is to embrace who you are fully—the culture, the love, and the creativity that define you. These universal languages will open doors, build connections, and create a legacy that transcends time and place. By understanding and using your gifts to help others, you'll find that the journey is about reaching your goals and making a meaningful impact on the world around you.

THE PATH FORWARD

I want to leave behind a message that art can turn adversity into strength and that by sharing our creativity with the world, we heal ourselves and create a community where everyone is valued and understood. My legacy is to remind people that creating and allowing others to create is a gift that extends far beyond the canvas—it touches lives and builds something far more lasting than a single piece of art: it builds a sense of purpose, hope, and connection.

I want people to see that no matter the obstacles, success is achievable when you remain true to yourself, your heritage, and your dreams.

My journey is a testament to the transformative power of art and the importance of using creativity not only as a personal outlet but also as a means to build community and foster well-being. Your unique background and experiences are your greatest strengths. By embracing these, you can create something meaningful that resonates with others and leaves a lasting impact.

My call to action is simple: Don't let fear or doubt hold you back. Whether you're just starting or reinventing yourself later in life, take that first step toward your dreams. Use your passions to uplift yourself and those around you. Remember that your story, heritage, and creativity can inspire and connect people in ways you might not even realize.

Together, we can create a legacy of empowerment, joy, and resilience that will continue to shine for generations to come.

ABOUT ANNIE

Annie Reyes, a dynamic Latina businesswoman with Cuban and Venezuelan roots, has built a remarkable career grounded in creativity, resilience, and a deep commitment to community. Growing up in Venezuela, Annie was profoundly influenced by her Cuban family, who instilled in her the values of hard work, determination, and the importance of professional education. Her dedication to marketing was recognized early in her career when she received the prestigious "Mara de Oro" award as Marketing Woman of the Year in Venezuela.

Despite her success, political turmoil in Venezuela led Annie to start anew in Miami, USA. Faced with language barriers and the challenges of adapting to a new environment, she overcame self-doubt and "impostor syndrome" to rebuild her career. In 2018, she joined the Kiwanis Club of Little Havana, eventually becoming Promotions Director and overseeing the marketing of major community projects and events, including the most prominent Latino festival in the U.S., the Calle Ocho Music Festival, and the well-known local art festival, Carnaval on the Mile.

In 2020, during the uncertainty brought on by the COVID-19 pandemic, Annie rediscovered her passion for art. This led her to create Hivedeco, a business that merges art and well-being, helping others cope with the challenges of the time through creative expression. She has since painted over 500 commissioned pieces of art and published more than ten coloring books, available on over 15 online platforms, both nationally and internationally, including Barnes & Noble, Walmart, and Amazon. Her work promotes relaxation, mental health, and a sense of community. In 2024, she earned her Certification in Art Therapy, was recognized as the Best Coloring Book Author in Florida, and was nominated for the Connecting Community Award by United Latinas Inc.

Annie's journey, especially in her 50s, demonstrates that pursuing your dreams is never too late. Her story is a testament to the power of embracing one's heritage, nurturing passions, and using creativity to build a legacy of connection and joy.

Learn more and connect with Annie at:

Website: www.hivedeco.com
Instagram: @HivedecobyAnnie
Facebook: Annie Reyes Art
Linkedin: Annie Reyes
Tik Tok: @annie.hivedeco

BEATRIZ ALBINI-RUIZ

"The journey begins with one courageous step. Your story, your success, and your impact are waiting for you to claim them."

-    Beatriz Albini-Ruiz

~ ~ ~

Beatriz Albini-Ruiz is more than a leadership coach—she is a trailblazer who transformed her immigrant journey into a powerful empowerment mission. Growing up in Colombia and arriving in the United States as a young adult, she confronted the challenges of adapting to a new culture and navigating the complex landscape of corporate America as a first-generation professional, turning her challenges into a roadmap for emerging leaders.

~ ~ ~

This chapter is dedicated to my sons, Sebastian and Rodrigo, and my husband, David, and my parents, who never stop believing in me.

.

.

BREAKING CYCLES, BUILDING LEGACIES: THE POWER OF BELIEF AND ACTION

THE JOURNEY

The path to where I am today was anything but easy.

As a dual business owner—running both a professional services firm and a high-end luxury retail candle brand—a homeowner and a real estate investor, I sometimes question, "How did I get here?" I even admit that a part of me feels extremely lucky. After all, how did a girl who came from Colombia at age 19, with just $700 in her pocket, make it this far?

The truth is, it took a lot more than luck. It required courage, grit, determination, focus, creativity, and an unwavering growth-oriented mindset. Every setback I encountered was not an actual setback but rather an

> *Every setback I encountered was not a true setback but rather an opportunity to test, validate, and create a new way forward.*

opportunity to test, validate, and create a new way forward—turning obstacles into stepping stones that would shape the journey ahead.

Looking back, for example, I remember my first month in the U.S. With dwindling funds and no prospects in sight for my preferred line of work at the time—childcare, as I was a trained assistant teacher—I decided I wasn't going to wait any longer for a job. I was going to make it happen. Armed with the ads section of a newspaper and a very heavy accent, I walked into every establishment listed with an "open house" until I finally found someone who would give me a chance.

That someone was Alistair, a red-haired GM who hired me as a barista at a two-star restaurant in Manhattan. The job came with late hours, physically demanding work and a toxic environment. I faced constant sexual harassment from colleagues and discrimination from both peers and patrons because of my accent. Yet, I look back at that first job with fondness because it taught me so much about myself and others.

At the same time, I was attending BMCC (Borough of Manhattan Community College), where I enrolled in an associate program in business. I juggled shifts and classes, pursuing my educational goals between long restaurant hours.

Thanks to that first job—and perhaps to the manager who took a chance on me—it ultimately inspired my career choice in human resources and professional development, which I do today. I realized early on that I had a deep need to inform and educate others so they wouldn't have to endure the same struggles I did.

Teaching runs in my blood—my grandmother was a teacher, my mother was a teacher, and so were my aunts. In a way, I've followed in their footsteps, but instead of teaching in a traditional classroom, I teach leadership, emotional intelligence, communication, and management.

I initially chose HR because I wanted to help workers like me understand their rights and advocate for themselves. However, as I gained more experience, I realized that I could make an even greater impact by educating leaders and aspiring leaders. That realization led me to focus on leadership development and executive coaching, where I could empower individuals at a larger scale—creating better workplaces and stronger organizations.

THE LEARNINGS

Fifteen years later, during the pandemic, I faced one of the biggest obstacles of my life. When the pandemic hit, I found myself without my corporate job, in a dead job market, and carrying a lot of responsibilities, including a shared mortgage and the care of my three-year-old son. To make matters worse, the way my employer and I parted ways was far from amicable. While I can't go into details due to settlement and legal issues, I can say that I declined to sign the release of rights and refused the initial severance offer. Against the advice of my family, I stood firm and chose not to sell my rights for the meager amount offered. This decision burned a bridge I had spent six years building, putting me in an incredibly tough spot.

During this turbulent time, I discovered the power of meditation and mindfulness for the first time. Amid all the chaos, mastering my thoughts became a crucial skill that gave me clarity and radical focus under immense pressure. I realized mindfulness didn't require sitting in a lotus position or long periods of meditation. For me, it came in the form of mindful breaks, like walking with my son and appreciating the gifts of nature.

Nature became my teacher. I started noticing how everything in nature has a purpose. A bird of prey uses its highly developed vision to spot food from incredible heights, while a whitetail rabbit uses its agility to dodge the bird's attack. Both are uniquely equipped to thrive. This observation sparked a realization: what if I could harness my strengths and create my own table instead of seeking a place at someone else's table?

The idea of flying solo as an entrepreneur terrified me. Growing up, I had seen my parents, who were independent operators, struggle with feast-or-famine cycles. The thought of abandoning the corporate success I had worked so hard to achieve—a stable, predictable income as a corporate leader—for a path full of uncertainty felt like an enormous leap. But as I continued practicing meditation and mindfulness, I found clarity about my next steps. I learned to listen to my inner voice and follow those intuitive nudges.

During one meditation, I had a moment of divine clarity. I heard a voice reminding me to trust the process and that I already had everything I needed to succeed. My life experiences, resourcefulness, grit, and determination had carried me through my early days in the States, and they could take me again. That voice urged me not to be afraid to toot my own horn and step boldly into my next chapter.

With that guidance, I made a pivotal decision: I stopped applying for HR roles and instead reached out to my network. I was no longer just a person seeking a job—I was someone whose unique life experiences, combined with my skills and abilities, held incredible value. I was ready to help others fulfill their leadership potential.

Taking another leap of faith, I reached out to the founders of SkillCycle (formerly GoCoach), whom I had known from my years as head of HR. I didn't have a perfect executive coaching résumé, nor did I hold the ICF credentials at the time. But, just as I had walked out of my aunt's house with a newspaper in hand years ago, I decided to ask and make a pitch for myself. To my delight, they said yes.

And just like that, I made my second career pivot. I became part of the coaches' bench at this incredible organization, and soon, other opportunities followed. This chapter of my journey reinforced a powerful truth: trust the process, believe in your values, and never be afraid to take a chance.

THE INSPIRATION

My great-grandmothers on my mom's side were both determined and entrepreneurial. They created their own luck—one opened a small convenience store, and the other started a bakery. Both women raised their families and elevated them from one societal level to another. My grandmother Blanca, also on my mom's side, was an elementary school teacher in rural Colombia, where she taught countless children how to read and write. In addition to raising seven children and teaching, she ventured into real estate. She used to flip properties, buy them, have them fixed, and then sell them for a higher price.

Book-wise, I have always loved Robert Kiyosaki's *Rich Dad, Poor Dad*. That book opened my eyes to the fact that there's more than one path to creating wealth. It also awakened in me an awareness of how cultural and mindset traps were playing a role in holding me back.

Over the years, I've also become a devoted student of stoic philosophy and a fan of Ryan Holiday's books. In particular, *The Obstacle Is the Way* has been instrumental in helping me navigate some of the most challenging moments in my journey, especially the ups and downs of entrepreneurship.

THE ADVICE

Looking back, I believe sometimes I waited too long to take action. I tolerated situations, not being proactive enough or holding back. Either to raise my hand for a promotion, push back on work that was not strategic, negotiate for more, or not interview for a higher-level role out of fear or self-doubt. Fear of rocking the boat, fear of not being likable, fear of not being perfect, fear of hearing no, fear of not saying the right thing—because I was not sure—fear of losing what seemed to be a comfortable situation financially but was not fulfilling nor helping me grow.

If I had to advise my younger self and others going into similar pivots in life, I would ensure to take action, even if the action is imperfect.

Don't get me wrong, I'm not encouraging anyone to do things in haste.

As I've grown older, I've learned that the only thing we can't get back is time. So, the more proactive we take action, even if imperfect, the better it is than wasting time tolerating situations. It does not have to be big actions; it can be as simple as starting with ourselves and changing how we think and approach life. We must know our values, strengths, weaknesses, and blind spots. The adage "know thyself" rings true now as it did back then.

I often hear, "Life happens"—and that might sound logical—but we have the power of choice, even when it seems like we don't. Yes, life happens, but you can also make it happen.

Lastly, trust the process. I'm the first one to admit that it is hard to embrace, but at some point in the game, when things are getting difficult, and we are hitting that rough patch, instead of playing the mental blame game, the best thing that we can do is release it and instead embrace a learning attitude. Because it's not "Why is this happening to me?" but "What is the lesson I need to learn here?"

THE PATH FORWARD

Success is not something we need to follow, it's something we can create and define for ourselves.

One message resonates deeply as I reflect on my journey, the challenges I've faced, and the lessons I've learned: success is not something we need to follow; it's something we can create and define for ourselves.

By knowing who we are, tuning inward, and committing to consistent, courageous actions, we have the power to design a life of purpose and fulfillment. Wellness and mindfulness aren't indulgences—they are tools that help us navigate the pressures and lows of life, enabling us to rise stronger, clearer, and more intentionally.

Too often, we remain stuck in roles or situations because we don't take action, don't communicate our needs, or don't recognize our own values. This leads to a life we merely tolerate, not one we purposefully design. But it doesn't have to be this way. Whether you are a Latina aspiring to climb the corporate ladder but feeling trapped in a role that undervalues your talents or a Latina trying to break free from the cycle of scarcity and self-doubt, know that it's possible to redefine your path. You can step into your own leadership identity—whether as a corporate leader or a small business owner. It's not about following someone else's recipe for success; it's about knowing and believing in yourself and taking those bold, intentional steps forward.

As a leadership coach, I've had the privilege of working with countless talented professionals, and one trend I see far too often—especially among Latinas—is self-doubt. The fear of not being good enough paralyzes many of us, whether as a mother, daughter, friend, or professional. This fear stops us from communicating our needs, taking risks, and "rocking the boat." But I want you to know that you are good enough. You are talented, capable, and worthy of success on your own terms.

I hope to inspire change and show other Latinas that taking a chance on yourself is not just possible but necessary. You can create a life that aligns with your dreams and values by embracing your unique talents, believing in your worth, and stepping into your power. The journey begins with one courageous step. Your story, success, and impact await you to claim them. Let's rewrite the narrative—together.

ABOUT BEATRIZ

Beatriz Albini-Ruiz is more than a leadership coach—she is a trailblazer who transformed her immigrant journey into a powerful empowerment mission. Growing up in Colombia and arriving in the United States as a young adult, she confronted the challenges of adapting to a new culture and navigating the complex landscape of corporate America as a first-generation professional, turning her challenges into a roadmap for emerging leaders.

As the CEO and founder of Brave Leadership Group, she has dedicated her career to empowering professionals to break through systemic barriers and unlock their full potential. Her work offers a holistic approach to leadership development that recognizes every individual's unique strengths and challenges. Working with global powerhouses like Google, SAP, and AT&T, Beatriz has become a catalyst for change, proving that diversity and individual potential are key drivers of innovative leadership.

A certified Professional Coach with credentials from the International Coach Federation and Cornell University, Beatriz embodies the transformative power of self-belief. Her philosophy is radical in its simplicity: every professional, regardless of background, carries within them the seeds of extraordinary leadership. Through her coaching, workshops, and mentorship, she helps high-performing talent redefine success on their own terms.

When she's not championing professional empowerment, Beatriz finds joy in her most important roles—as a mother, wife, and keeper of her cultural traditions, often found in her kitchen preparing authentic Colombian arepas or tending to her garden, nurturing growth both metaphorical and literal.

Learn more and connect with Beatriz at:
Company Contact: https://www.braveleadershipgroup.com/
Personal Coaching: https://www.beatrizalbiniruizcoaching.com/

CECILIA COSSIO

"Head up, Shoulders Back! Go Be In Your Greatness!."

\- Cecilia Cossio

~ ~ ~

Cecilia Cossio is a dynamic leader, entrepreneur, real estate investor and advocate for women's empowerment, known for her passion for creating opportunities and building a lasting legacy. As the founder and CEO of NexGen Legacy, Cecilia leads a company dedicated to transforming the real estate landscape by delivering sustainable solutions that impact investors, communities, and generations to come. With over 30 years of experience in real estate asset management and development, she has become a trailblazer in a predominantly male-dominated industry, specializing in affordable housing and multifamily investments.

~ ~ ~

To my kids and grandkids, who are my greatest inspiration and the reason I strive to create a legacy of strength, love, and opportunity. And to my grandparents, whose unwavering love, sacrifices, and lessons of resilience laid the foundation for everything I am today. This is for you.

AUTHENTICITY, PERSEVERANCE, IMPACT: THE KEYS TO BUILDING A LEGACY

THE JOURNEY

Growing up in a tightly knit Mexican family, my journey was shaped by a deep sense of connection, cultural pride, and an unwavering belief in the importance of family. My grandparents, who raised me, were the bedrock of my values. They exemplified generosity and hard work, often sacrificing their needs to ensure their family could thrive. Watching them navigate life with dignity and resilience planted the seeds for my own determination to create change.

From a young age, I knew I couldn't settle for anything less than my best. When I wanted to learn gymnastics, but my grandparents couldn't afford lessons, I taught myself how to do back handsprings in their front yard. In that same yard, I experienced the pain of watching my family get evicted and then was sent down the street to play with my friends so I wouldn't see the heartbreak unfold. These moments taught me the value of perseverance and self-reliance. They also ignited a determination to break the cycles of struggle and create a stable foundation for my future.

Another formative experience was growing up in a household where my aunts and uncles often bickered instead of lifting each other up. I saw how deeply that hurt my grandparents, who only wanted harmony within their family. From this, I learned the importance of fostering unity and teaching my children to support one another rather than tear each other down. Watching my grandfather break his back to ensure I didn't have to live the life the rest of our family experienced stayed with me even as I became a mother myself. His sacrifices and unyielding work ethic became a model for how I approached my own life and challenges.

One pivotal turning point in my life came as a teenager. I struggled with the duality of my identity—feeling "not Latina enough" for some and "too

Latina" for others. It was a constant push and pull, leaving me to question where I belonged. I realized, however, that my uniqueness was my strength. This perspective grew stronger when I became a mother at 18. The challenges of raising a child while navigating societal judgment were immense, but they taught me responsibility, resilience, and the power of purpose.

A key moment in my life was my entry into the multifamily housing industry. Initially, I felt out of place, entering rooms where people didn't look like me or believe I belonged. But instead of retreating, I leaned into those moments. I educated myself, asked questions, and refused to be underestimated. Over time, I moved from feeling invisible to being a force for change, challenging the norms and creating spaces where others could feel empowered.

Both the positive and negative experiences in my life have played critical roles in shaping who I am today. The joy of family festivals in my grandparents' backyard taught me the importance of community, while the pain of being underestimated fueled my desire to prove my worth. These experiences culminated in a mindset that values both grit and grace—the grit to push through barriers and the grace to lift others along the way.

My background and upbringing gave me a foundation rooted in faith, resilience, and the drive to leave a legacy. My grandparents' love and sacrifices taught me that life is not just about individual success but about creating opportunities for those who come after us. This understanding drives my work as a changemaker, ensuring that the doors I open remain open for others to walk through.

Today, as the Founder and CEO of NexGen Legacy, I lead multiple business branches, including Legacy Real Estate & Asset Management, Legacy Consulting & Contracting, and CGP Legacy Roofing & Construction. My work centers on overseeing multifamily property portfolios focused on affordable and workforce housing solutions, consulting with investors and developers to create sustainable communities, and advancing housing initiatives for workforce members, seniors, and veterans.

Beyond this, I'm deeply passionate about mentoring women and minorities in the real estate space, sharing my story through speaking engagements, podcasts, and books like ReWIRE: Real Women in Real Estate. I'm also preparing to launch my podcast, *The Power of You*, to ignite conversations about housing, community, and individual value that creates a lasting impact for future generations.

THE LEARNINGS

Life's greatest challenges have often been my greatest teachers. I've had several defining moments, but aside from childhood trauma, I believe my failed marriages had the greatest impact on me.

As a young mother of two in a difficult marriage, I faced the enormous weight of family expectations. In our culture, staying together was often prioritized over personal happiness, and for years, I tried to hold on for the sake of appearances. It wasn't until I realized the cost of that decision—to my self-worth and my children's well-being—that I found the strength to leave. Walking away was one of the hardest but most transformative decisions I've ever made.

Another turning point came during my second divorce. The guilt of another failed marriage weighed heavily on me, especially as I tried to explain it to my three children. This time was different because we had a son who brought a new light into our lives. Unlike with my first two children, with whom I grew up as they did, this time, I had the maturity to fully understand the impact of my choices. This marriage ended due to an illness that is often misunderstood and, in our culture, widely accepted—but I knew I couldn't accept it. It felt like a generational curse that allowed my value to be defined by others, and I knew it had to be broken.

A change occurred when I decided to invest in a mastermind and educational program. Once again, I found myself in a room of investors who didn't recognize my worth. I had decided to sit back—until I couldn't. I spoke up, sharing what I knew to be true from my experience in multifamily commercial real estate investment.

At that moment I realized, "You can invest, but if you don't know how to operate your investment, it means nothing." I realized what I had been doing for 27 years was indeed my superpower!

That moment shifted everything because I realized my superpower and vowed never to look back. From that day forward, I have embraced my worth and used it to create a legacy for myself and those who come after me.

I overcame these hurdles through a combination of faith, self-reflection, and the support of key individuals who believed in me when I struggled to believe in myself. This has led to my desire to disrupt systems that perpetuate inequality, advocate for diversity and inclusion, and create pathways for others to succeed.

Every challenge, every barrier I have broken and continue to forge through, is a reminder of the power we hold when we refuse to be limited by others' perceptions.

THE INSPIRATION

My inspiration stems from the people, faith, and cultural values that have shaped my life. My grandparents were my first and most enduring source of inspiration. Despite their financial struggles, they created a nurturing environment filled with love, hard work, and resilience. Their influence taught me the dignity of perseverance, a lesson deeply rooted in our Hispanic heritage.

Becoming a mother at 18 reshaped my priorities. My children and grandchildren became my "why," motivating me to push through challenges and build a legacy for future generations. I wanted to show them—and others—that success is possible regardless of where you start.

Faith has also been a cornerstone of my journey. Prayer and reflection gave me the strength to navigate life's darkest moments, from toxic relationships to career transitions. These moments of clarity reinforced my belief that struggles have purpose and better days are ahead.

Mentors played a crucial role, offering guidance and wisdom when I needed it most. Each mentor taught me a unique lesson—whether it was simplifying success, embracing my strengths, or navigating challenges with grace. Their support reminded me of the importance of investing in others.

Today, my inspiration has evolved. It's not just about survival; it's about creating spaces where others can thrive. My heritage reminds me of the power of community and collaboration, and I strive to honor those values through mentorship, leadership, and advocacy

THE ADVICE

Looking back, if I could offer advice to my younger self, it would be this: First, focus on creating your own legacy. Remember that your faith in God will carry you through the worst times. No matter how much you want to grow your career, always prioritize spending time with your children—it is what truly matters most. Trust the process. Every challenge, every setback, is preparing you for something greater.

Embrace your boldness, because being outspoken is not a flaw — it is your superpower.

Always remember, your worth is not determined by others' opinions but by your unwavering belief in your own potential. Embrace your boldness, because being outspoken is not a flaw—it is your superpower.

I'd remind myself that failure is not the opposite of success but a critical part of it. Mistakes are not moments to fear; they are opportunities to grow. I would tell my younger self to set boundaries earlier—to protect her peace, prioritize self-care, and do so without guilt. And most importantly, I'd tell her not to let anyone who looks down on her define her value. The only critic that can hold you back is yourself, so speak to yourself with the same compassion and encouragement you'd offer to someone you love.

To anyone going through a similar journey, know this: the forces meant to keep you down will whisper ugly things to make you doubt yourself. But listen to your heartbeat—it is yours, steady and unstoppable, a reminder that you are designed to be greater than anything the world throws your way. When you walk into a room, and others are intimidated by your presence, it's because God created you to be powerful and limitless. When you walk in His greatness, your greatness shines through.

Growing up as a Latina, I often felt caught between worlds—too Mexican for some, not Mexican enough for others. That struggle with identity could have consumed me, but instead, it taught me the strength of authenticity. I'd remind my younger self that she didn't need

> *The struggle with identity could have consumed me, but instead, it taught me the strength of authenticity.*

to conform to anyone's expectations to succeed. Her unique story, resilience, and heritage are her greatest strengths. Those moments of brokenness—being a teen mom, navigating Section 8, or enduring toxic relationships—were not endings but beginnings. They shaped the determination and empathy that define who I am today.

To anyone facing similar challenges: Your circumstances do not define your destiny. Hold on to your faith, remember your "why," and never stop dreaming. Your story matters, and every step forward, no matter how small, is progress. Surround yourself with people who see your potential and seek mentors who can guide you through uncharted territory.

Practical habits like journaling, prayer, and continuous learning have been instrumental in my growth, helping me reflect, recharge, and stay grounded in my purpose. Cultivating gratitude has been transformative, shifting my focus from challenges to blessings.

Finally, I'd tell my younger self—and you—that you are enough. You were created for greatness. The road ahead will have challenges, but each one will prepare you for something extraordinary. Walk boldly, set boundaries, embrace your heritage, and shine. You are limitless, and make your table that you and others like you can sit at. Never allow anyone to make you feel like less because you are great!

THE PATH FORWARD

The legacy I hope to inspire in others through my story is one of resilience, empowerment, and the courage to rewrite their narrative. My journey is a testament to the fact that where you start does not define where you can go.

I want others, especially women who feel overlooked or underestimated, to see that they, too, can break barriers, shatter stereotypes, and create meaningful change in their lives and communities.

The legacy I aim to leave is rooted in three core principles: authenticity, perseverance, and impact. First, I want people to understand the power of authenticity. You don't have to fit into someone else's mold to succeed—You have Greatness within you designed JUST FOR YOU. Your unique story, strengths, and struggles make you capable of achieving greatness. By embracing your true self and owning your journey, you unlock the ability to inspire and connect with others on a deeper level.

Second, I want to inspire perseverance. Life will throw challenges your way, and it's easy to feel defeated by failure, trauma, or self-doubt. My story is a reminder that failure is not the end—it's a stepping stone. You can rise above your circumstances and use them as fuel to drive your growth. Whether it's surviving financial instability, navigating toxic relationships, or overcoming personal insecurities, the key is to keep going. Take small steps forward, even when the path seems unclear.

Finally, I want my legacy to inspire others to create an impact that reaches beyond themselves. True success isn't just about what you achieve—it's about what you give back. I hope my life as a mom and grandma, my work in affordable housing, mentorship, and leadership exemplifies how we can all use our strengths to lift others. My ultimate goal is to leave the world better than I found it by creating spaces and opportunities where everyone can thrive regardless of their background.

My message to everyone reading my story is simple: don't let fear or doubt stop you from pursuing your dreams. You are more capable than you realize, and the world needs what only YOU can offer. Start by believing in yourself and taking the first step, no matter how small it may seem. Surround yourself with people who uplift you and align with your vision, and don't hesitate to walk away from those who drain your energy.

I challenge you to reframe your mindset when faced with adversity. Instead of asking, "Why is this happening to me?" ask, "What can I learn from this?" Shift your focus from what's holding you back to what's propelling you forward. Every setback has the potential to teach you something valuable, and every obstacle is an opportunity to grow stronger.

If you've been blessed with the ability to overcome, I urge you to pay it forward. Share your story, mentor others, and create opportunities for those who come after you. Remember, your legacy isn't just about what you accomplish; it's about how you make others feel and the doors you open for them.

Together, we can build a legacy that inspires future generations to dream bigger, work harder, and believe in themselves. Your story matters. Your voice matters. And your impact will ripple far beyond anything you can imagine. Let's create a world where everyone has the chance to live with dignity, strength, and purpose. Be in Your Greatness to Help Others Live in Their Greatness!

ABOUT CECILIA

Cecilia Cossio is a dynamic leader, entrepreneur, real estate investor and advocate for women's empowerment, known for her passion for creating opportunities and building a lasting legacy. As the founder and CEO of NexGen Legacy, Cecilia leads a company dedicated to transforming the real estate landscape by delivering sustainable solutions that impact investors, communities, and generations to come. With over 30 years of experience in real estate asset management and development, she has become a trailblazer in a predominantly male-dominated industry, specializing in affordable housing and multifamily investments.

Cecilia's story is one of resilience, grit, and vision. From being a teen mom and navigating the challenges of early motherhood to building a thriving career and earning a seat at the table as an investor and business owner, she embodies the strength and determination that define extraordinary leadership. Her chapter in *Extraordinary Latinas* and her contributions to the *REWIRE* series reflect her unwavering commitment to helping other women break barriers, dream big, and achieve their fullest potential.

A passionate advocate for diversity, equity, and inclusion, Cecilia actively mentors women of color, empowering them to embrace their unique strengths and pursue their dreams fearlessly. She believes in the power of mindset, authenticity, and collaboration to drive success while inspiring others to create a legacy that transcends their lifetime.

Beyond her professional achievements, Cecilia is a proud mother, grandmother, author, and speaker. She strives to balance her work with faith and family values, leaving a profound impact on the lives she touches.

Learn more and connect with Cecilia at:
Website: nexgenlegacy.com
Instagram: Iamceciliacossio
LinkedIn: linkedin.com/in/ceciliacastillocossio

DORA MENDEZ

'My purpose is to enrich lives through People, Culture, Wellness, and Joy!

-   Dora Mendez

~ ~ ~

Dora Mendez, MPA (she/her/ella), Founder and CEO of Coach Dora LLC, and C-Suite Executive with 12+ years of human resources (HR) experience. Her mission is to be a beacon of bold authenticity, igniting conversations on diversity, equity, and inclusion (DEI) through her writing and public speaking. She envisions a world where everyone feels empowered to lead with courage and compassion, and her leadership Coaching and Human Resources consulting services are the tools to make this vision a reality.

~ ~ ~

To my children, Naomi and Mateo, you inspire me everyday.

¡UNIDOS!
A CELEBRATION OF AFRO-LATINIDAD

THE JOURNEY

My Intersectional Identity - Afro-Latina Mami and Entrepreneur

I am a cisgender, Afro-Latina, entrepreneur, wife, mother, and lifelong New York. I moved from the neighborhood of Hell's Kitchen in midtown Manhattan to Harlem in upper Manhattan in 2011, when I met my now husband, Dylan Rogers.

For 12 years, my family and I called Harlem home, just two blocks from the Arturo Schomburg Center for Research in Black Culture[1]. Living in proximity to a cultural treasure trove allowed me to immerse my children in the rich legacy of Arturo Schomburg, an Afro-Puerto Rican historian whose profound impact on preserving African and African diasporic contributions to history resonates deeply with me. Having earned a Bachelor's Degree in history with a concentration in Sub-Saharan Africa and later a Master's Degree in Public Administration, Schomburg stands as one of my heroes - an Afro-Puerto Rican trailblazer.

While my family and I celebrate Black history and Latinx[2] heritage every day, the focused attention during Black History Month in February and Hispanic & Latinx Heritage Month from September 15th to October 15th annually serves as an enriching tradition that strengthens our familial bonds and contributes to our children's inclusive education.

---

(1) The Schomburg Center for Research in Black Culture in Harlem, one of The New York Public Library's renowned research libraries, is a world-leading cultural institution devoted to the research, preservation, and exhibition of materials focused on African American, African Diaspora, and African experiences. https://www.nypl.org/locations/schomburg

It was at the Schomburg Center where we visited the Black Comic Book Heroes, Writers, and Illustrators exhibit. My son was six years old at the time, and his joyful exuberance at the unveiling of the process from sketches to comic books to superhero movies was unforgettable. The exhibit exposed how to bring one's imagination to life, inspiring him through his favorite Afro-Latino superhero, Marvel's Miles Morales, Spiderman. This exhibit became a highlight for our children, sparking engaging conversations about art, representation, and creativity.

Professionally, I'm known as Coach Dora, Founder & CEO of Coach Dora LLC, a People and Culture leader. However, the most important title for me is that of Mami. Raising my children to understand the importance of preserving and celebrating the diverse contributions of the African and African diasporic communities is my highest priority.

As my children mature, they actively participate in decision-making regarding our cultural and family activities. Encouraging their involvement allows my husband and me to shape our celebrations to their evolving interests and insights.

For example, when my daughter was ten years old, she was thrilled to learn about Celia Cruz in music class. Celia Cruz's music, filled with vibrant rhythms and powerful lyrics, captured her imagination and introduced her to a rich cultural heritage. Moreover, Celia Cruz, the "Queen of Salsa," became the first Afro-Latina featured on U.S. currency in 2024[3].

---

(2) Latinx: This term emerged as a gender-neutral alternative to "Latino" and "Latina," aiming to be inclusive of non-binary and gender non-conforming individuals. However, its usage has been controversial. The debate over this term reflects broader discussions about identity, inclusivity, and language evolution. While awareness of "Latinx" has grown, only a small percentage of U.S. Hispanics use it to describe themselves.

(3) The 2024 Celia Cruz Quarter is the 14th coin in the American Women Quarters™ Program. Celia Cruz was a Cuban-American singer, cultural icon, and one of the most popular Latin artists of the 20th century.

Cruz's image graces the reverse of the American Women Quarters™ Program coin. Exposing children to Afro-Latina figures like Cruz inspires a sense of pride in their cultural identity and fosters a deeper understanding of their ancestors' contributions to society.

By challenging the myth of a monolithic Latinidad, I emphasize the importance of recognizing and embracing the beauty of our rich cultural diversity.

As Coach Dora, a Human Resources (HR) & Diversity, Equity, and Inclusion (DEI) consultant, I appreciate the opportunity to share my story of embracing authenticity and inclusive leadership. As an Afro-Latina People & Culture leader, I share powerful examples of Afro-Latinx trailblazers and how diverse experiences within the Latinx community have helped me overcome adversity. By challenging the myth of a monolithic Latinidad, I emphasize the importance of recognizing and embracing the beauty of our rich cultural diversity.

THE LEARNINGS

The reality that Latinas make up less than 2% of the C-suite is unfortunate[4]. This is why the world needs books like this anthology. Our authorship is an investment in supporting the amazing talent that Latinas have to offer. We are examples, not exceptions, of how to lead by overcoming adversity. If we can be successful Entrepreneurs and Executives, you can too!

The impact I wish to create is to inspire other Latinas to have the confidence to lead with courage and compassion. Navigating a career in HR, especially within the nonprofit sector, can indeed present unique challenges. My experience sheds light on the complexities of diversity, equity, and inclusion (DEI).

---

(4) Only three Latinas have been CEO of a Fortune 500 company. In 2017, former PG&E CEO Geisha Williams became the first. https://leanin.org/article/first-latina-ceo-fortune-500#

Let's delve into my journey and explore how I overcame these obstacles:

1. **Naivety and Nonprofit Realities**:
   It's common to enter a new field with idealistic expectations. Assuming that the nonprofit sector would uniformly embrace DEI was a testament to my passion and optimism. However, the reality is often more nuanced. Like any other organization, nonprofits can have varying levels of commitment to DEI. Some may fully align with the mission, while others may lag behind. Overcoming this challenge required a shift in perspective. Recognizing that change takes time and persistence allowed me to adapt and find alternative ways to drive DEI initiatives.

2. **Navigating Stereotypes**:
   The stereotype of the "Angry Black Woman" is unfortunately pervasive. It unfairly labels assertive Black women as aggressive or confrontational. My ability to navigate this stereotype speaks to resilience and self-awareness. I had to strike a delicate balance between assertiveness and avoiding reinforcement of the stereotype. The emotional labor of navigating the "Angry Black Woman" stereotype in the workplace, especially among my lighter-skinned Latina colleagues and contemporaries, is often ignored or dismissed. I hope sharing my experiences in this chapter will empower others facing similar challenges. This chapter is a starting point for openly discussing colorism and identity within the US Latinx community. I aspire to break down harmful stereotypes as a champion of inclusion.

3. **Inner Strength and Coping Mechanisms**:
   Finding inner strength during challenging times is crucial. Reflecting on moments when I drew upon resilience, determination, and self-belief has been essential. Coping mechanisms can vary from unhealthy to healthy, so it's important to find constructive

   Recognizing your worth and the value you bring to the table is essential. Celebrate your achievements and acknowledge your growth.

coping methods by turning to mentors, mindfulness practices, or hobbies. I use nightly journaling to unburden my thoughts so I can rest, and this practice of gratitude helps me stay grounded and focused. Recognizing your worth and the value you bring to the table is essential. Celebrate your achievements and acknowledge your growth.

4. **Support Systems**:
Whether it was colleagues, mentors, friends, family, or a faith-based community, having a network to lean on during tough times has made a significant difference. That motivates my podcast *Building Leadership Community* (YouTube: @coachdoram). It can be lonely at the top, but it doesn't have to be. Sometimes, navigating challenges alone can be isolating, and sharing experiences or seeking advice from others who've faced similar situations can be invaluable. United Latinas has provided an online community space to network and find support.

5. **Challenging Norms and Disrupting the Status Quo**:
As an Afro-Latina People & Culture leader, I've challenged established norms and systems. Reflecting on my advocacy for change within organizations and the HR profession, I eventually pivoted my career to set my entrepreneurial spirit free and start my own business, Coach Dora LLC.

THE INSPIRATION

My leadership journey began with *Familia* – my parents, both civic-minded leaders who raised my two sisters and me in the Hell's Kitchen community in midtown Manhattan (now known as "Clinton").

My father, John Mendez, may he rest in peace, passed away in September 2021 due to complications from Covid-19. Daddy was a proud Puerto Rican and Army veteran. A Vietnam Veteran and recipient of two Purple Hearts, he dedicated nearly three decades to military service with the National Guard and Army Reserves. His dedication and resilience taught me the importance of service and perseverance.

My mother, Zenaida Mendez[5], immigrated from the Dominican Republic when she was 14 years old. Mami, an Afro-Latina women's rights trailblazer, has devoted her life and career to amplifying the voices of women, LGBTQI+ individuals, and other marginalized communities.

She works in community media to uplift the voices of the voiceless, providing a platform for free and independent storytelling. Her passion for advocacy and social justice has earned her numerous accolades and awards. My mother's work has deeply influenced my values and commitment to making a difference. Growing up in a household where discussions around speaking truth to power were common, I experienced several pivotal moments that shaped my journey.

Witnessing my father's bravery and my mother's relentless fight for gender equality instilled in me a strong sense of responsibility to continue my parents' legacy. I hope to set a similar example for my own children. Overcoming personal challenges and setbacks has also strengthened my resolve and empathy, enabling me to connect with and support others facing similar struggles.

My "DominiNuyorican" background and civic-minded upbringing provided a strong foundation of resilience, empathy, and a commitment to social justice. These experiences have shaped the person I am today, driving me to be an empowering changemaker in my community.

---

(5) Blog post to learn more about "Celebrating Zenaida Mendez: A Women's Rights Trailblazer" https://www.coachdoramendez.com/news-and-articles/zenaida-mendez

THE ADVICE

On my podcast, "Building Leadership Community," I consistently ask every guest: "What advice would you give your younger self? What essential knowledge should the next generation of leaders possess to thrive?" As I reflect on these questions, three core principles emerge:

1. **Prioritize Wealth Building:** From the moment you begin earning, initiate retirement savings. Had I commenced retirement contributions at 21 instead of 30, I would undoubtedly have accumulated greater wealth. The perception that retirement planning is solely for the distant future is a misconception. Regardless of the contribution amount, consistently saving at least 10% of your income is paramount – an investment in your secure future[6].

2. **Cultivate Supportive Networks:** Don't go it alone. Avoid loneliness and isolation by actively building a community of individuals who will uplift and empower you. Embrace the power of diverse perspectives and inclusive teams. My co-authors and the community of UNITED LATINAS [7] are a perfect example of how a supportive network of diverse perspectives can inspire and propel you to realize your dreams.

3. **Embrace a Growth Mindset:** Cultivate adaptability and flexibility. The capacity for continuous learning and improvement to evolve, and navigate unforeseen circumstances is crucial for navigating the complexities of leadership in an ever-changing world.

I believe these principles offer valuable guidance for aspiring leaders, fostering a foundation for success built on financial security, collaborative relationships, and the resilience to thrive in a dynamic environment.

---

(6) Qualitatively I lost out on $40,000 in interest and employer matching funds. Employer matching fund means free money if you take advantage of this benefit. As an HR executive, I have shared this with new hires and entry level staff.

(7) www.unitedlatinas.com for more information on how to join this community of Latinas and their allies

THE PATH FORWARD

Your journey is not only about overcoming challenges but about making a meaningful impact on a more equitable and inclusive world. Each step you take contributes to a future where all voices are heard, respected, and valued.

My mission is to be a bold advocate for authenticity, leading critical conversations on Diversity, Equity, and Inclusion (DEI) through my writing and speaking. I believe that true leadership is rooted in courage, compassion, and the celebration of every identity. Inclusive leadership means valuing all contributions, and together, we hold the power to create change.

Join me in building a stronger, unified future—where inclusion is the foundation for achieving our personal and professional dreams. Let's move forward, together – ¡Unidos!

ABOUT DORA

Dora Mendez, MPA (she/her/ella), Founder and CEO of Coach Dora LLC, and C-Suite Executive with 12+ years of human resources experience. Her mission is to be a beacon of bold authenticity, igniting conversations on diversity, equity, and inclusion (DEI) through her writing and public speaking. She envisions a world where everyone feels empowered to lead with courage and compassion, and her leadership Coaching and Human Resources consulting services are the tools to make this vision a reality.

Her leadership positions include Vice President of Human Resources & Chief Diversity Equity and Inclusion Officer and Director of HR roles at mission-driven non-profit organizations. Before this, she was in public service, utilizing her bilingual (English & Spanish) skills to investigate hundreds of employment and housing discrimination complaints.

Dora earned her Master's in Public Administration (MPA) at the City University of NY-John Jay College of Criminal Justice, and after graduation now teaching for 15+ years at John Jay as an Adjunct Professor.

As a lifelong New Yorker, she resides in NY with her husband and two children.

Learn more and connect with Dora at:
Website: https://www.coachdoramendez.com/
Linkedin: https://www.linkedin.com/in/coachdoram/
Instagram: https://www.instagram.com/coachdoram/
YouTube: https://www.youtube.com/@coachdoram

ERIKA DOX-MARTINEZ

"You deserve to live and fund the Blissful Vida you desire."

- Erika Dox-Martinez

~ ~ ~

Erika Dox-Martinez's journey from financial stress to empowerment inspires her mission to help others create lives filled with financial bliss, abundance, and freedom. As a financial wellness coach and founder of Blissful Vida LLC, she is dedicated to helping women and allies become more intentional, confident, and at peace with their finances. With a background in financial services and a Trauma of Money certification, Erika combines practical strategies with mindset work to help her clients overcome limiting beliefs, heal their relationship with money and achieve their version of financial bliss!

~ ~ ~

To my husband, whose belief in my vision and unwavering support make everything possible—this chapter is here because of your generous heart.
IFLY!
To my family, friends, and fellow Jefas, thank you for seeing me, believing in me, and cheering on my dreams.
To my ancestors, whose resilience and dreams live on through me – this is in honor of you.
And to all the littles in my family, even the big ones, may you realize sooner than I did that your wildest dreams are within reach and that you have everything within you to achieve them.
Lastly, my heartfelt gratitude to United Latinas for the opportunity to contribute to such an inspiring project alongside other extraordinary Latinas!

REDEFINING LATINA, REIMAGINING FINANCIAL BLISS

THE JOURNEY

I was born in New York City, a proud second-generation Puerto Rican. My parents separated when I was just two years old, and I grew up with my mom and stepfather in a household where Spanish wasn't spoken often. My connection to the language mainly came from my grandparents. When we spent time together, we found ways to bridge the language gap—I responded mainly in English, while they primarily spoke in Spanish. I understood un poquito de Español, but not being fluent led to feeling "in between."

Even at a young age, I noticed how lighter-skinned Latinos, like myself, were sometimes teased for "not being Latino enough." Comments about being "too white" planted early seeds of self-doubt about my identity. I even wanted to use my mother's last name, Gonzalez, so people would immediately recognize me as Latina. I started to feel like I didn't fully belong in my own culture, which lingered as I grew older.

When I went to college, those insecurities only grew stronger. I joined a Latino student organization, hoping to connect and find a sense of community. Instead, I felt judged for not fitting the mold of what others expected a Latina to be. Feeling disheartened, I stepped away from that organization and decided to move forward.

I focused instead on working hard, getting good grades, and securing a good job so I could, as my dad would say, "make the big bucks." I grew up thinking that was the definition of success and the path to avoiding the struggles so many people like us endured. So, with resilience and determination, I graduated from college and made my way into the corporate world.

Working in corporate, I quickly realized how rare it was to see other Latinos, especially women, in the spaces I occupied. It was sometimes isolating, and I often felt like I didn't belong. That began to shift when a fellow employee introduced me to a Latino Organization called ALPFA (Association of Latino Professionals for America). Walking into that community for the first time, I felt like I'd found my people. The negativity I'd experienced in the past about not "looking Latina" or speaking Spanish fluently was replaced by a sense of true belonging. For the first time in a long time, I felt accepted for exactly who I was, and that sense of acceptance helped me embrace myself. It helped me to learn that I wouldn't always be judged for not feeling Latina enough, and maybe, just maybe, I was judging myself!

Being part of that organization helped me realize that being Latina isn't about meeting a checklist of attributes—it's about owning your identity and celebrating where you come from. I let go of the idea that I needed to look a certain way or speak perfect Spanish to claim my heritage. Instead, I embraced my family's legacy, understanding that even though I didn't grow up like my grandparents and they're no longer with me, I carry their strength and honor them through my journey, values, and the life I'm building.

As I've grown older, I've learned that no one else can define me. I've fully embraced my identity—whether others recognize it or not. Now, I proudly connect with organizations like United Latinas, We All Grow Amigahood, Cafecito con Jefas and ALPFA, where I feel accepted and supported. I know that the feeling of "not being Latina enough" is something many in our community struggle with, and I want my story to resonate with readers who might feel the same. We all deserve to step into our full identity without letting others define us.

While I embraced my identity and connected with communities that truly uplifted me, there was still a part of me that felt unsettled. For years, I carried a persistent feeling that I was meant for something more than my career in financial services. Despite the whispers of that calling, I tried to silence those thoughts, reminding myself to be grateful for the stability and income my job provided. But no matter how hard I pushed them aside, the feeling lingered. But as life would have it, it has a way of nudging us toward the paths we're meant to take and sometimes in the most unexpected and challenging ways.

On 11/11/11, I was diagnosed with large granular lymphocytic leukemia (LGLL), a rare and chronic form of blood cancer that affects the immune system. Though I haven't been sick enough to need treatment, living with a chronic illness has been a constant reminder of life's unpredictability. Initially, the diagnosis brought fear and uncertainty, but it also sparked a shift in how I viewed my future. I realized I wanted more from life than simply following a traditional path—I wanted to make an impact and live with greater intention.

Since my diagnosis, I've been heavily involved with the Leukemia & Lymphoma Society (LLS) as we're relentless for a cure! Fundraising for them and supporting others in the fight gave me a renewed sense of purpose and showed me how powerful it is to turn challenges into action. Doing this meaningful work planted a seed: I wanted to dedicate my life to helping others while carving out a path that was true to me. Over time, this desire led me to leave the corporate world and pursue entrepreneurship, where I could create meaningful change and take control of my future. My diagnosis wasn't just a challenge; it became a catalyst for change.

It took some time but the changes really came about during the pandemic when I embarked on a journey of self-reflection. I seeked out therapy and dove into personal development and growth, allowing me to examine my life, values, and long-term vision, and the one thing that kept circling my mind was how unfulfilled I was working at my nine-to-five.

While unsuccessfully trying to pivot into the non-profit sector, I decided to take matters into my own hands. I realized I could make a real difference in others' lives by helping them with a challenge that I had overcome - finally taking control of my dinero!

My finances were in great shape in 2022, and I amassed over half a million dollars in net worth, but that wasn't always the case. My transformation from financial turmoil to financial freedom helped me to embark on my journey to becoming a financial wellness coach. This journey wasn't linear or easy, but every twist and turn has given me the wisdom, resilience, and purpose I carry today.

The spark that I didn't realize ignited it all was a transformation journey. In 2012, I got engaged to Jose, my now amazing husband! Amid the excitement, reality hit hard as I realized we had no savings to pay for a wedding, and I was in a mountain of debt. That moment of panic forced me to face my finances seriously for the first time. I felt embarrassed, stressed, and frustrated, mainly because I was making "good" money! It didn't make "cents" - ha! That AHA moment woke me up, and I decided not to walk down the aisle until we could cover the wedding costs in cash, as I didn't want to go into more debt just because we were getting married.

I poured myself into learning everything I could about budgeting, debt management, and saving. I had to make sacrifices here and there, but it was worth it because, by the time Jose and I finally got married in 2015, we saved $20,000 for our wedding and honeymoon, and I was well on my way to becoming debt-free.

This achievement was more than just a win for our wedding budget. It was my first taste of financial control and confidence. Within a year of saying "I do," I had completely eliminated my debt. I still remember the overwhelming relief of seeing that zero balance and realizing I had freed up over $1,500 a month. That money was no longer tied to the past. It was mine to save for a rainy day, explore investing, and start building wealth on my terms. This wasn't just a milestone, it was my version of financial freedom!

Like myself, I know many others who did all the "right" things, like go to college and get a good-paying job, thinking "we've made it." Yet they're still struggling with managing their money. They're not intentionally building wealth as most don't know where their money is going and don't have much to show for how much they make. They don't feel in control of their money either, and I thought, why not help them relieve financial stress and create financial success too?!?!

We aren't meant just to survive; we are meant to live in abundance and to thrive! It is our birthright!

We aren't meant just to survive; we are meant to live in abundance and to thrive! It is our birthright!

With that belief and desire, Blissful Vida was born out of my mission to help Latinas and women professionals take control of their finances and reach their fullest potential. Today, I help others overcome their financial struggles, reimagine their relationship with money, and achieve financial peace of mind so they can live and fund the blissful vidas they desire and deserve! This decision came with a lot of hesitation and fear, but I knew that I was meant for more and pushed through to start my own business, eventually leave my nine-to-five, and trust the process!

Many of the women I serve make "good money" but still feel stuck or uncertain about where it's all going, just like I did. Some are overwhelmed by debt or unsure how to save consistently, while others want to manage their money more effectively to align with their long-term goals. Whether they're striving to break free from financial stress or building greater confidence and clarity, I'm here to guide them toward a healthier, more intentional relationship with money.

What makes Blissful Vida unique is our trauma-informed approach to financial wellness. As a Trauma of Money-certified coach, I understand that financial struggles are often tied to unexamined money stories and emotional wounds—patterns rooted in past experiences or trauma. My work goes beyond the numbers by helping women heal these hidden barriers and shift from scarcity to abundance in both mindset and practice. Assisting clients to rewrite their 'money stories' to see money as a tool for freedom rather than stress is one of the most fulfilling parts of my work.

Through my journey, I've learned that embracing your identity, overcoming challenges, and creating meaningful change are interconnected. From navigating the complexities of cultural identity to confronting financial struggles and health challenges, every step has led me to a place of purpose and empowerment. Blissful Vida is not just a business; it's a reflection of my personal transformation and a commitment to helping others experience the same.

I want every woman who reads this to know that financial freedom, self-confidence, and a life of abundance are possible—no matter where you start. Our journeys may not be linear, and fear may try to hold us back, but we can achieve extraordinary things with resilience, intention, and a willingness to heal.

THE LEARNINGS

Transforming myself from an accountant—someone who often worked quietly behind a desk with limited interaction—to becoming Blissful Vida's vibrant, visible face was one of the most significant challenges I've faced.

The journey wasn't just about building a business but about stepping into a version of myself I'd never envisioned. This transition required me to work on new skills and push through deep-seated public speaking and visibility fears. Suddenly, I was hosting workshops, speaking on podcasts, and leading engagements that pushed me far out of my comfort zone. Each of these roles demanded a level of openness and vulnerability that was initially daunting but ultimately essential for showing up fully for my mission and purpose.

One of the most profound struggles was the decision to leave a stable, six-figure job to pursue Blissful Vida full-time. While I had the savings to support myself, walking away from the steady paycheck I'd grown accustomed to brought waves of doubt and fear.

I knew entrepreneurship wouldn't provide the same predictable income, and facing that uncertainty was intimidating. For some in my family, leaving a secure job, especially one that offered a reliable income, seemed risky—even reckless. Their concerns stemmed from a place of love and care, but it made the final step to leave that much harder. When those closest to you feel uneasy, it's easy to let that amplify your own doubts, but I reminded myself that my vision for Blissful Vida was worth taking the leap.

Finding the inner strength to move forward required me to cultivate unwavering trust in myself and my mission. To stay grounded, I anchored myself in the bigger purpose behind Blissful Vida: to redefine how we approach financial well-being by blending strategy with personal empowerment. This holistic perspective not only sets Blissful Vida apart but also challenges traditional narratives around money, encouraging people to view financial health as a cornerstone of overall wellness and a catalyst for meaningful change.

Shifting my focus from personal fears to the impact my work could have on others gave me the courage to persevere, even when the path felt uncertain. Embracing the idea of collective transformation over individual gain became a powerful source of motivation and a constant reminder of why this work matters.

I also found it helpful to seek out mentors and coaches, along with immersing myself in entrepreneurial communities. Having the guidance of those who had navigated similar transitions was invaluable. They understood the complexities of leaving a "safe" path and showed me that courage isn't about eliminating fear but moving forward despite it. Fellow entrepreneurs offered insights and encouragement that helped me stay grounded through the ups and downs. These relationships became anchors, reminding me that every entrepreneur faces moments of fear and uncertainty and that stepping into the unknown is essential to building something meaningful.

THE INSPIRATION

My journey to achieve financial bliss was deeply influenced by my family's financial habits and the narratives I grew up with. My parents separated when I was young, and growing up, I saw two distinct financial approaches from each of them. They each worked hard to provide, yet their experiences revealed certain limiting beliefs about money that are still common in our communities.

Whenever money was tight, my dad would sometimes say it was because we are "Poor-Ricans" (Poor Puerto Ricans), emphasizing that financial struggle was an inevitable part of life for people like us. While he may have meant it in a lighthearted way, it echoed a message that scarcity was our norm and that financial freedom wasn't in the cards for us. This label became ingrained in me and shaped my early perception that money would always be a source of stress and limitation. I carried that mindset forward for a long time, unconsciously believing that financial peace and success were meant for others, not for me.

My mom didn't call us that, but she had her own financial baggage that I had to unpack as I got older. While I don't remember her being stressed about money, I noticed she used credit cards often. Without realizing it, I adopted this habit myself, assuming that using credit was an acceptable way to manage everyday expenses. By the time I graduated college, my credit card debt was pretty hefty, and I had a lot of student loans, too! Even after I started working and eventually made six figures (a "good" income), I still lived paycheck to paycheck and struggled with managing my money because I was never taught how.

I realize that my parents did their best, and I'm grateful for them, but when I had my financial wake-up call, I was inspired to leave those financial narratives behind and change my money story to one of empowerment! I forgave myself for getting into debt and let go of the notion that we're just meant to struggle with money because we're "Poor-Ricans." I decided that those weren't my stories to keep and that I would move forward in a way where I could use money as a tool to build wealth and finally make it work for me! And I did, and that inspired me to believe that I also had the power to guide and coach others to do the same, so I bet on myself and started Blissful Vida!

Taking the leap into entrepreneurship was a big shift for me. No one in my family had ever owned a business, so I didn't have an example to follow. To find the courage to take this step, I leaned on the wisdom from one of my favorite books, *The Alchemist* by Paulo Coelho. The book's messages about pursuing one's "personal legend" and trusting that the universe supports us in our journey spoke directly to my heart. It mirrors my path with Blissful Vida, reminding me and those I work with that when we commit to our goals, the universe truly does align to support our endeavors.

The universe has blessed me on this journey with the support of my loved ones and, at the correct times, some fantastic mentors, coaches and amigas! I am part of a few communities, and without their support and guidance, I'm not sure how far I would be because sometimes it's a lonely road. But these relationships have provided me with invaluable strength and accountability as I've navigated the highs and lows of building a business. I'm incredibly grateful for the people who truly embrace me and my essence; their encouragement is also a great source of inspiration for me.

THE ADVICE

Reflecting on my journey, there are several pieces of advice I'd give to my younger self and anyone walking a similar path. Funny enough, I still need this advice today, but I wish I had taken it in a lot sooner.

1. **Never underestimate the power of speaking up for yourself.**
   For years, I hesitated to ask questions or put myself out there, fearing judgment or rejection. Early in my entrepreneurship journey, I attended an event where, despite my nerves, I gathered the courage to raise my hand and ask a question. That single act of bravery opened a door I hadn't anticipated. It led to a conversation with someone influential at the event, eventually resulting in an opportunity to lead a financial wellness workshop and a long-term collaboration. This experience taught me that sometimes, it takes one moment of courage to set a new path in motion. For anyone holding back out of fear, I encourage you to push through and speak up. Your voice is your power, even if it's shaky, and the opportunities it brings can be life-changing.

2. **Release the need for perfection.**
   This is something I still struggle with, so I'm taking this advice alongside you all. Progress is what moves you forward, not perfection. Whether in business or personal growth, focusing on perfect execution often holds us back. I learned that I didn't need everything to be flawless before sharing it with the world. Each "imperfect" step forward was progress, teaching me more than if I had waited for the perfect moment. When you let go of perfectionism, you give yourself the freedom to learn, evolve, adapt, and take meaningful action—qualities that are essential for growth in any venture.

3. **Cultivate awareness as the foundation for transformation.**
   Awareness is key to understanding where you are, where you want to go, and why. At Blissful Vida, we encourage awareness as the first step in any journey to financial wellness. Uncovering your money stories and knowing exactly where your money is going are key, so you can start making intentional choices that align with your goals and values. Consider creating a "Blissful Spending Plan." Unlike traditional budgeting, which often feels restrictive, this approach puts you in charge of giving every dollar a purpose or a job—whether it's paying your bills, saving, investing, or spending on things that bring you bliss! Embracing awareness in this way empowers you to align your financial behaviors with your aspirations, making your money a tool for well-being and progress rather than a source of stress.

> *Uncovering your money stories and knowing exactly where your money is going are key, so you can start making intentional choices that align with your goals and values.*

THE PATH FORWARD

I want to inspire a legacy of empowerment, resilience, and financial independence, especially among Latinas. My story proves that transformation is possible no matter where you start, and a holistic blissful vida is attainable.

Let this be a call to action for you: to speak up for yourself, embrace the challenges of growth, and to pursue your blissful dreams with unyielding courage. Do not be daunted by the fear of the unknown. Like turning the pages of a book, each step you take opens up new possibilities.

I urge you to begin by examining your own money stories—those narratives that have shaped your relationship with money, for better or worse. Challenge them, rewrite them, and take control of your financial future. Remember, your ordinary actions can lead to extraordinary outcomes.

Together, let's turn the hope of a blissful vida into a reality for everyone and generations to come. We truly deserve it!

ABOUT ERIKA

With over two decades of experience in the financial service sector and a transformative personal journey, Erika is the visionary founder of *Blissful Vida*. Her mission is clear: to empower women and allies to achieve financial peace of mind and a life of true abundance and bliss.

Erika's path to financial wellness coaching began with her own challenges—navigating debt and financial overwhelm. She overcame these hurdles through determination and strategic planning, igniting a deep passion to help others rewrite their financial stories. She's dedicated to simplifying financial complexities and empowering her clients to build a confident and fulfilling financial future.

At *Blissful Vida*, Erika leads a revolutionary approach to financial wellness by integrating the emotional and spiritual aspects of money with practical strategies. From cultivating an abundance mindset to crafting blissful spending plans and mastering saving and investing, she helps her clients achieve holistic financial transformation.

Erika's mission is to empower others to overcome financial stress, transform their relationship with money, take control of their finances, and achieve financial peace of mind—aka bliss.

She believes that financial mastery is a right, not a privilege. Her approach blends compassion, expertise, and actionable strategies to illuminate the path to a *Blissful Vida*—where financial empowerment and holistic well-being come together seamlessly.

If you're ready to break free from financial stress and embrace a life of abundance and bliss, Erika is your trusted guide to financial transformation and a brighter future.

Learn more and connect with Erika at:
Linkedin: https://www.linkedin.com/in/erika-dox-martinez/
Website: https://www.myblissfulvida.com/

As a special gift for readers, Erika is offering her *Shift Your Money Mindset Workbook*—a powerful resource designed to help you break free from the money stories and limiting beliefs holding you back from living your financially blissful vida!

Download your free copy
here: https://www.myblissfulvida.com/moneymindset

GEORGINA DIAZ

"Setbacks are temporary, and perseverance always leads to growth."

Georgina Diaz

~ ~ ~

Gina Diaz is a resilient attorney who has overcome incredible challenges. Determined to help immigrants find solutions to their difficulties, she opened her firm, Diaz Case Law more than 10 years ago. She understands her clients' unique challenges and what it means to have someone in your corner when times are tough.

~ ~ ~

FROM FEAR TO FREEDOM: EMBRACING LIFE'S SILVER LININGS

THE JOURNEY

I came to the United States with my mom when I was just five years old, and my dad had already come ahead of us. I remember being deported two or three times, though, at the time, I thought we were just going back and forth on field trips. My parents came here with nothing but the clothes on their backs, and they worked tirelessly to provide a better life for us. My mom and dad's sacrifices shaped who I am, and I understand my clients' struggles because I've lived them. I'm not just the daughter of immigrants—I am an immigrant myself.

We settled in Little Village, Chicago. It wasn't a wealthy suburban neighborhood, but it was home, and I loved it. My parents worked in factories their whole lives, instilling in me the value of hard work. My mom took on a factory job to pay for my private school education. She poured her entire paycheck into my tuition, leaving herself with maybe $20 or $30 after each payday. Her sacrifices showed me the transformative power of education and the lengths she was willing to go for my future. Seeing this sacrifice made me realize that if my mother was willing to work this hard so I could go to school, then I'd better make it count.

When I was 19, I found out I was pregnant. It was a huge blow to my family, especially since I'm an only child in a traditional Mexican household. In our Catholic family, being an unmarried pregnant teenager was not what any parent would hope for their only daughter. I had my daughter at 20, and although my parents were not happy about the situation, they welcomed her with open arms and became my biggest supporters.

I didn't let that challenge stop me from striving for a better future—for them and for my daughter. I kept moving forward, working full-time while attending school at night to become a paralegal. My days were long and exhausting; I would wake up early, work a 9-to-5 corporate job in downtown

Chicago, take the train and bus to my night classes, return home late to help care for my daughter, complete my homework, and catch just a few hours of sleep before starting all over again. It was tough, but I knew it was the only way to build the life I envisioned for us.

Eventually, I realized I wanted—and could—do more. I set my sights on becoming a lawyer. My family was skeptical; law school was expensive, and we didn't have the money. But I was determined to find a way. Despite not knowing anything about the process, I applied for scholarships and loans, determined to make it happen.

Leaving my daughter with my parents, I moved to Michigan to attend law school. I fast-tracked my degree by taking extra classes and finished in just two and a half years. Every weekend, I would drive back home to spend time with my daughter and parents, and whenever they needed me, I made the trip without hesitation. It was grueling, but I pushed through, graduated, and embarked on my career.

In 2008, during the economic downturn, and with the unwavering support of my family and my then-boyfriend (now husband), I took a leap and started my law practice. I combined immigration law with real estate and even became a real estate agent, working alongside my husband. I loved helping my community and felt that I was giving back in my own small way.

Thankfully, my firm grew quickly, and I felt on top of the world. I also got married and welcomed two more beautiful daughters into my life during this time. It felt like a dream come true.

But just when I thought I had it all, life had other plans. At just 32 years old, I was diagnosed with ovarian cancer. My youngest daughter was less than a year old, and I was still hoping to have more children—at least one more, maybe even a boy, I thought. The news shattered me. I underwent multiple surgeries, including a complete hysterectomy, which meant I would never be able to have more children. Losing that part of myself sent me into a dark place.

I would never experience pregnancy again or have the son I had hoped for. The irony wasn't lost on me. At 19, I hadn't wanted to be pregnant, and now at 32, when I truly wished for another child, that possibility was taken away. Life has a strange way of unfolding.

While I was battling cancer, my business partner embezzled money and nearly destroyed my firm. I had to take out loans just to keep it afloat. For a while, I was consumed by anger—anger at God, the world, my circumstances, and even myself. I was drowning in self-pity, blaming God, my shady business partner, and everything in between.

But then, one day, everything changed. I don't know exactly why or what triggered the shift, but I'm so grateful it did. That morning, I woke up, looked in the mirror, and realized I couldn't keep living like that. I decided to change my perspective and recognize the blessing I had been given. Instead of asking, *"Why me?"* I started saying, *"Thank you for another chance."*

Ovarian cancer—often called *The Silent Killer*—and yet here I was...ALIVE! Wow. I had no other cancer in my body, no need for radiation or chemotherapy, and I was still here. What in the world was I angry for? I looked at myself and thought, *"Snap out of it and start living the life granted to you!"*

That moment changed everything for me. I committed to focusing on the good, even amid challenges. I realized that life is a gift, and every day I wake up is an opportunity to make a difference. I learned to embrace challenges as lessons and to approach life with gratitude and optimism. Now, I remind myself and others that fear only holds us back, and our perspective shapes our reality. My journey has taught me that while we can't always control what happens to us, we can control how we respond—which makes all the difference.

THE LEARNINGS

I've always tried to see the cup as half full, focusing on the silver linings and positives in life. Every choice we make leads us in a direction, and I'd rather make choices that guide me toward something good than dwell on the negative. Life doesn't always go as planned, but that's okay. When challenges arise, you learn, adjust, and move forward. If we never fail, how can we succeed?

Trying and failing is far better than not trying at all.

One of the most significant lessons I've learned is about fear. Fear is a powerful force that paralyzes or propels us forward. Often, we fear what we don't know, but once we step into that unknown, we realize it's not as intimidating as we imagined. Fear can be a friend, signaling growth and new opportunities. I've come to see fear as a motivator—something that, when overcome, brings a deep sense of pride and accomplishment. Even failure isn't something to fear because every failure is a lesson. Trying and failing is far better than not trying at all.

For example, the fear I felt after my cancer diagnosis was overwhelming, but it also forced me to face my mortality and think about what legacy I wanted to leave for my family. That fear was the driving force behind building a better financial foundation for my children and parents. The fear of thinking that I would leave this world and my family wouldn't be financially stable without me pushed me to start building wealth and leaving a legacy for my family. It motivated my husband and me to dive into real estate investing— a path that has provided us with stability and allowed us to grow and give back to others. Through real estate investing, we have found the stability and "wealth" that gives me peace of mind and assures me my family will be taken care of should God decide to take me out of this world. So I no longer have that terrible fear.

Mentorship has also been crucial in my journey. When I set a goal, I seek out people who have already achieved what I aspire to. Early on, I realized that listening to advice from those who haven't walked the path I want to follow can lead to stagnation. Instead, I've learned to surround myself with people who live the message they preach. Andrew Holmes, one of my greatest mentors, guided my husband and me as we built a sizable real estate portfolio. His guidance showed us how to take calculated risks and approach every deal with strategy and confidence. We learned how to overcome the fear of being a "landlord" and dive into the possibilities instead. Keila.

Resilience has been at the heart of everything I do. From juggling night school and a full-time job while raising my daughter as a single mom to

Setbacks are temporary, and perseverance always leads to growth.

rebuilding my business after betrayal, I've learned to rise above challenges with determination. These experiences have shaped my mindset: setbacks are temporary, and perseverance always leads to growth.

Finally, I've learned that success requires action, perseverance, and surrounding yourself with the right people. Talk is cheap, but taking action and sitting at the table with those you aspire to emulate will open doors. Life won't hand you opportunities—you have to claim them. Don't let fear or doubt stop you. A seat at the table is waiting for you; you just have to go out and take it.

THE INSPIRATION

Inspiration has always been a driving force in my journey, and it comes from so many places. I've learned to embrace the mindset that anything is possible if you commit and work towards it. Growing up as a Latina, I often saw how societal and cultural expectations tried to define what we could or couldn't do. But I've always believed that those perceived limitations are opportunities—what some may see as obstacles, I've learned to see as advantages.

Sharing my story has become another source of inspiration. I didn't think my experiences were unique enough to share for years, but every time I opened up about my journey, I saw how it resonated with others. Hearing people say, "I've been through something similar," or "Your story helped me see what's possible," made me realize the importance of vulnerability. That's why I'm committed to being open about my challenges and how I overcame them.

I also find inspiration in the people I've encountered and the lessons they've taught me. Mentors and role models—those who are living examples of success—have shown me the importance of perseverance and learning from others who have walked the path before you. This is especially true in my real estate journey. The guidance of those with experience helped me build a legacy for my family, something I never imagined was within my reach.

Finally, my own life experiences continue to inspire me. Surviving ovarian cancer at 32 was a turning point. It forced me to rethink everything and recognize the preciousness of life. It taught me to find the silver lining, no matter how hard things get. Even fear, which once felt like a barrier, has become something I see as a companion—an indicator that I'm about to step into something new and potentially life-changing.

To me, inspiration is everywhere. It's in the people who believe in you, the lessons life throws your way, and even the struggles you never thought you'd face. It's about seeing every moment as an opportunity to grow, learn, and help others do the same.

THE ADVICE

Investing in real estate is something I firmly believe in. Real estate is one of the safest investments you can make, and you shouldn't let anyone tell you otherwise just because they failed at it. Often, failure comes from not doing it the right way. Look into it—if you study some of the richest people in the world, you'll find they all have a sizable real estate portfolio. It's a solid way to build wealth if you approach it correctly.

The second piece of advice is simple but powerful: believe in yourself. If you don't believe in yourself, how can you expect others to? Too often, we are our own biggest critics, doubting ourselves and letting those doubts hold us back. But when you walk into a room knowing you belong there, people will sense it. If you walk in unsure, thinking, *What if they don't like me? What if I don't belong here?*—that's exactly what people will pick up on.

So, every day, look in the mirror and remind yourself *I am amazing. I am beautiful. I am smart. I am confident. I've got this.* Cheer yourself on, because if you don't, who will? I know it might sound corny, but trust me—it works. I've been stuck in my own head during some of the darkest times in my life.

Staying in that negative mindset only kept me there. It wasn't until I started changing how I saw myself that I noticed how people around me changed, too. It wasn't that they thought I was what I feared I was; it was that they finally saw me as I saw myself.

Finally, trust your gut. Your instincts are powerful and often guide you in the right direction. Don't doubt yourself. Love yourself, believe in yourself, and trust yourself—because once you do, the world will see you the way you see yourself.

THE PATH FORWARD

If there's one message I want to leave with anyone reading this, you can do anything you want as long as you commit and work toward it. Especially as Latinas, we often grow up in a culture that unintentionally sets limits on what we believe we can achieve. But I've learned that what some might see as obstacles—being a woman and being a minority—are advantages when we embrace them fully and work hard to meet our goals. Everything happens for a reason, you just have to see it.

I've always believed in starting with the end goal and working backward to create a clear path. Life will always throw challenges your way, but every challenge is an opportunity to find the silver lining. The cup is always half full if you choose to see it that way. I've found so much strength in flipping what others might consider setbacks into the very tools that propel me forward.

Looking ahead, I'm excited about the freedom I've worked so hard to create. My oldest daughter is about to graduate from law school, and I'm thrilled to watch her step into her own career. My younger daughters still need my guidance, but I'm looking forward to traveling and truly enjoying life. I get to decide what I want to do for the first time—not because I have to, but because it brings me joy. That's the greatest blessing, to live life on your terms.

I don't have a specific roadmap for what's next because I trust that whatever God has planned for me will be exactly what I need. I hope that by sharing my journey—honestly and openly—I can help others see their own potential.

If even one person finds a spark of inspiration or feels less alone because of my story, then it's all worth it. We're here to uplift and support each other, to show what's possible when we commit to our dreams and help each other along the way.

For me, the future isn't about slowing down—it's about doing what fulfills me and helps others. That's what I'm excited about: to keep growing, sharing, and making an impact, however big or small, on the lives of others. Life keeps getting better when you approach it with gratitude, determination, and the belief that you're exactly where you're meant to be.

ABOUT GEORGINA

Gina Diaz is a resilient attorney who has overcome incredible challenges. Determined to help immigrants find solutions to their difficulties, she opened her firm, Diaz Case Law more than 10 years ago. She understands her clients' unique challenges and what it means to have someone in your corner when times are tough.

Gina immigrated to the United States with her family from Mexico when she was five and was returned twice with her mother before they were able to successfully enter the US and she was able to start school. Not understanding the language in a new school can be scary, but Gina learned that if she could overcome that, she could do anything if she was willing to work for it and not let fear get in the way.

That "I can do anything if I work hard" attitude became Gina's philosophy as she overcame many obstacles in her life. She became a single mother at 19, working days at a law firm and attending college at night to earn her bachelor's degree. Gina knew that the sacrifices her family had made to live in the US couldn't be in vain.

While working at the law firm, Gina discovered her passion for law and her mission, to help people, whether they are undocumented immigrants, facing foreclosure, investing in real estate, or starting a business. She knew that helping others would be rewarding and joyful.

She went to law school, opened her law firm, and after having her third child, was diagnosed with ovarian cancer at the age of 33. In another twist of fate, and once again proving her resilience, Gina had to rebuild her business after a trusted partner destroyed it while she was fighting for her life. She says that all she has been through proves that miracles do happen when you conquer fear.

Gina has become one of the top immigration and real estate attorneys in Chicagoland. Her love for real estate added another dimension to her law practice as clients come to her for foreclosure defense, seeking ways to keep their homes, loan modifications, and short sales.

Gina began building her real estate empire by purchasing and rehabbing properties for herself. After expanding her real estate portfolio, she began giving back as one of the founding members of We Win, LLC, an organization dedicated to introducing women to the world of real estate, and We Win, NFP, a not-for-profit that is transforming lives while providing transitional housing to strengthen communities.

Learn more and connect with Gina at:

Linkedin: https://www.linkedin.com/in/georginadiaz1/
Website: https://www.diazcase.com/

GLADYS RODRIGUEZ-PARKER, MS

"When the door is closed because you're not wanted at the table, open it and take your seat! ."

- Gladys Rodriguez-Parker

~ ~ ~

Gladys's story reflects the rich and diverse heritage that has shaped her identity and worldview. As a Jibara from Cerro Gordo, San Lorenzo in Puerto Rico, she was raised with a deep connection to her roots, drawing strength from the Taino, African, and Spanish influences that have shaped her culture and community. The Jibara identity, often linked to rural Puerto Rican traditions, emphasizes self-reliance, resilience, and a strong sense of family.

Her family's move to South Boston, Massachusetts, during a time of social and racial turbulence added another layer to her personal narrative. The experiences of racism and discrimination that Gladys faced as part of the Puerto Rican diaspora in the United States would undoubtedly have had a profound impact on her worldview. These challenges likely instilled in her a strong sense of justice and a commitment to fighting for civil rights, human rights, and social equity.

~ ~ ~

For my husband Steve, my sons Carlos and Jonathan and my grandchildren Yani, Jonah and Xavier. To the family I played with in the Batey and to the ancestors who worked in the fields and loved unconditionally. To Congressman James P. McGovern, my friend, and for being a fierce advocate, leader, and overall good guy!

FROM THE FOGÓN TO THE TABLE:
A LIFE OF SERVICE AND STRENGTH

THE JOURNEY

My story begins in Cerro Gordo, nestled within the majestic central mountain range of San Lorenzo, Puerto Rico. It's a place where the mountains rise like ancient sentinels, and the *fogón*—the hearth—serves as the lifeblood of our existence. My childhood was a tapestry woven from the rhythms of rural life, cradled in the warmth of family and the soil we tilled. My *Abuelo*, Pedro Rodriguez, was a master carpenter, and his skilled hands measured not just wood but dreams. He presided over a farm that welcomed not only his children but also their families, including my seven brothers and parents. My cousins were my closest playmates, and together, the farm was our boundless universe. We embraced our identity as *Jíbaros*—countryside dwellers farming the land with time-honored traditions. Although our material wealth was scant, we overflowed with love, interconnectedness, and a steadfast sense of community underpinned by the rhythm of hard work.

It's essential for me to share that I embody three distinct yet intertwined identities as a Puerto Rican: I am Spanish, *Taino*, and African—a beautiful mélange of peoples who carry the weight of history, bearing the scars of conquest, massacre, and enslavement.

But by the 1960s, the world I cherished began to crumble. The Puerto Rican economy had diverged sharply from agriculture, and families like mine found it increasingly difficult to survive off the land. I learned early on about hunger and food insecurity, realities that shaped my understanding of survival. In 1969, my family made the wrenching decision to leave our island home behind, setting our sights on the mainland in search of brighter prospects.

We arrived in Boston on a frigid February morning, unprepared for the merciless winter that awaited us. The chill was a stark awakening, a physical manifestation of the hurdles looming in our future. At Logan Airport, we staggered onto the icy tarmac, clad in thin, inadequate clothing. The wind pierced through my skin, and I faced the biting chill of uncertainty for the first time.

Our first home was a cramped studio on Broadway Street, where ten of us squeezed into a single room, sharing the space like a puzzle crafted by necessity. We slept on the floor and took turns in the small kitchen, swiftly realizing the sacrifices this new journey would demand. For weeks, we stayed indoors, shackled by our lack of winter gear, yearning for warmth.

Hope flickered one Sunday morning when my mother, Maria, spotted the steeple of a local church piercing the gray sky. After attending services, she bravely introduced herself to a group of nuns. That very afternoon, these nuns—dressed in their flowing habits—brought food, blankets, warm clothing, and sturdy boots. They secured us a new home at the Old Colony Housing Projects on D Street in South Boston. For the first time on the mainland, I savored the joy of having my own room—a space that was distinctly mine, complete with a bed and a desk where I could write. Yet, D Street was far from a sanctuary; it was fraught with danger based on racism and discrimination. Hostility and violence greeted our family at every turn, scaring our dreams of safety.

On New Year's Eve 1970, that hostility erupted into terror when Molotov cocktails shattered our fragile sense of security, hurtling into our apartment. We narrowly escaped with our lives, fleeing to Worcester, Massachusetts, with nothing but the clothes clinging to our backs. Today, that horrifying act against my family would echo through the halls of justice as a hate crime, leaving an indelible mark of trauma.

Worcester became our new home, but the struggles were relentless. Despite being a seventh grader at heart, I was placed in the fourth grade, trapped in a foreign language that twisted my tongue and left me vulnerable. The language barrier became a double-edged sword, a source of bullying as classmates hurled slurs and fists at me and my brothers. Yet amidst that tumult, I began to find my voice. I battled for my rightful place in school, challenging the principal to evaluate my capabilities in Spanish and thus proving that I belonged. That victory marked the genesis of my lifelong quest for justice.

Education transformed from a mere refuge into my salvation. I developed an insatiable love for learning that continues to this day. Despite the challenges of becoming a single mother in high school, I refused to let my circumstances dictate my future. With unwavering support from mentors and sheer determination, I graduated from North High School. In the fall of 1975, I carried my son on my shoulders, a backpack bursting with books, as I bravely embarked on my journey at the University of Massachusetts, Amherst.

The road was anything but smooth; financial struggles, exhaustion, and societal pressures often threatened to overwhelm me. Yet, each class, each step forward, reminded me of what was at stake. I craved more—not just for myself but especially for my son, Carlos. Over time, my passion for education emerged as a guiding light, stirring a calling to serve and advocate for justice.

Sharing those precious moments at our kitchen table and doing homework side by side with my son was profoundly powerful. It was a testament to the value of learning, a bond forged through shared aspirations and hope.

Completing my History and Political Science degree at UMass and Worcester State University became the catalyst for roles that cemented my identity as an advocate and leader. My first significant foray into leadership began when *Padre Miguel Bafaro* invited me to serve as the executive director of Centro Las Americas in Worcester. At that time, Centro Las Americas stood alone as the only Latino organization in the city, grappling with scarce resources and a lack of visibility. I embraced the challenge with fierce determination, recognizing it was more than just a job—it was a mission to uplift my community.

At Centro Las Americas, I dedicated myself to transforming the organization into a beacon of empowerment for the Latino community. We pioneered programs for children, establishing a homework center dedicated to supporting their education, while also launching the first program for elderly Latinos—a space for connection and care. We opened a homeless shelter for women and children, fiercely advocating for systemic change and spearheading initiatives to retain bilingual education in Worcester's public schools. This mission was not merely about addressing immediate needs but laying the groundwork for enduring change. During my tenure, I had the honor of helping create Worcester's inaugural Latin American Festival, a vibrant celebration that continues to illuminate the cultural landscape today. We understood the power of civic engagement, and on festival day, we set up a voter registration site—a challenging endeavor given Worcester's stringent requirements.

After five years at Centro Las Americas, I transitioned to serve as the Director of Minority Affairs at UMass Medical School. In this capacity, I crafted pathways for underrepresented students in medicine, nursing, and biomedical sciences. I developed programs exposing high school students to careers in health sciences, supporting their pursuit of higher education. My time at UMass was about bridging gaps between students and opportunities and between institutions and communities. Witnessing young people step into previously excluded spaces was deeply fulfilling, knowing I had opened doors for them.

When Jim McGovern won his election in November 1996 to represent Massachusetts's 3rd Congressional District, none of us could have anticipated the profound impact he would have on my life—or I on his. Brought on as his district director, I stepped into a transformative role, igniting my passion and commitment to the communities we served. My mission became clear: to ensure that Congressman McGovern's office radiated hope, addressing an array of issues—from health care and social security to education, immigration, civil rights, and veterans' advocacy. Each challenge we faced became an opportunity to realign destinies and foster real change in the lives of those we represented.

As the first Puerto Rican woman to hold such a prominent position in the Massachusetts delegation, I felt honored and a sense of responsibility to rise to the occasion. Congressman McGovern's unwavering support became my anchor, fortifying my resolve to serve with integrity and passion. For nearly three decades, I worked tirelessly to ensure his office became a refuge of hope for all constituents. Whether I was representing him at national events or advocating for local concerns, every action resonated with my lifelong commitment to justice and equity.

I vividly remember the moment a girl from Cerro Gordo stepped into the hallowed halls of Congress, badge hanging around my neck, feeling the weight of history pressing down upon me. Sharing that life-changing experience with my mother—a proud migrant worker and housekeeper— was a moment etched into my soul, uniting us in a tapestry of dreams come true. It was a gathering of diverse hearts and minds, converging in the People's House for a momentous occasion.

Contrast that with the chilling events of January 6th, 2021, when a mob stormed the United States Capitol, unraveling the fabric of democracy itself. Chaos erupted as they overran Capitol Police, desecrating property and endangering the lives of elected officials like Vice President Mike Pence and Speaker Nancy Pelosi. Watching that horrifying spectacle unfold on national television was gut-wrenching. Congressman McGovern, now chair of the Rules Committee, was a pillar of strength, ensuring every member exited the chamber safely before he stepped outside, only to confront a throng of rioters trying to breach the House chamber's doors. This was not the peaceful transfer of power we envisioned—a cornerstone of our democracy, a graphic contrast to the traumatic events in countries whose democratic futures remain uncertain.

In this role, I discovered the essence of service and what it truly means to witness history—both the inspiring and the terrifying—and the unwavering journey towards a more just and equitable society.

Every role I undertook—at Centro Las Americas, UMass Medical School, and alongside Congressman McGovern—was a continuation of my journey. I traveled a path defined by service, resilience, and the passionate belief that one person can ignite change. These roles were not just jobs; they were my calling.

THE LEARNINGS

Looking back on my life, I've learned countless lessons, each born from both triumph and hardship. These are three of the most profound:

1. Resilience is Built Through Adversity

Life's challenges are inevitable, but do not define you—your response does. My family's journey from Puerto Rico to the mainland, the loss of everything we owned, and the uphill battles in education and society taught me this: resilience is a muscle. You strengthen it every time you rise after falling. There were countless moments when I wanted to give up—when the weight of being a single mother, a

> *Life's challenges are inevitable, but they do not define you – your response does.*

student, and an activist felt too heavy. Yet, each step forward made me stronger and more determined to carve a path for myself and those who would follow.

I've learned that resilience often requires accepting help. Early in my journey, I struggled with the notion that asking for help was a sign of weakness. But over time, I realized that it takes courage to lean on others, to admit when you can't carry the load alone. Whether it was my mother stepping in to care for my son while I studied, a mentor-writing a check for a much-needed suit, or a community rallying behind Centro las America's programs, I learned that resilience is not just personal—it is collective. It grows when we draw strength from each other.

2. Justice Requires Relentless Pursuit

From an early age, I recognized the injustices around me. Whether it was being placed in the wrong grade because of my language, seeing my brothers bullied for their identity, or witnessing systemic inequities in education and housing, I felt a deep sense of responsibility to act. Justice is not passive; it demands action. It's about showing up, speaking out, and refusing to accept the status quo.

One of the most pivotal lessons I've learned about justice is that it's a marathon, not a sprint. It requires patience, persistence, and the willingness to endure setbacks. There were moments in my work at Centro las Americas and later in public service when progress felt agonizingly slow. Systemic change doesn't happen overnight. But the small victories—establishing a bilingual education program, funding a community homework center, or opening doors for underrepresented students in medicine—reminded me that every step forward matters. Justice is cumulative, built on the shoulders of those who came before and paving the way for those who will follow.

3. Community is Your Strength

I owe so much of my success to the community that surrounded me. From my mother's unwavering support to the mentors who guided me, the neighbors who helped us find housing, and the activists who fought alongside me, I've learned that no one succeeds alone. Community is a foundation, a wellspring of strength that propels you forward even when the road seems impassable.

Community extends beyond shared geography – it's about shared purpose.

Through my journey, I've learned that the concept of community extends beyond shared geography— it's about shared purpose. At Centro las Americas, I witnessed how people who didn't have much themselves still showed up to help others, donating time, energy, and resources to lift the entire community. Similarly, in my work with Congressman McGovern, I saw how a united community could rally for policy changes that benefited everyone, from improving housing conditions to advocating for healthcare reform. Community is not just about receiving support; it's about giving it in return, creating a cycle of empowerment and solidarity.

4. Education is the Great Equalizer

Perhaps one of the most transformative lessons I've learned is the power of education. It was through education that I found my voice, my purpose, and my path to leadership. However, I also learned that access to education is not equal, and systemic barriers often keep the most marginalized from reaching their full potential. This is why I have dedicated so much of my career to advocating for bilingual education, creating pathways for underrepresented students, and mentoring young people who, like me, faced steep odds.

Education is not just about degrees and credentials—it's about opening minds, challenging assumptions, and fostering the skills needed to create change. It is a tool of empowerment, one that has the potential to break cycles of poverty and inequity. My journey from a struggling student to a university graduate and community leader is a testament to what education can do for individuals and entire communities.

Each of these lessons has been hard-won, shaped by the trials and triumphs of my life. They are not abstract ideals but lived truths, guiding me as I continue to navigate the complexities of justice, leadership, and service. I carry them with me as reflections of the past and as tools for the future.

THE INSPIRATION

During my darkest hours, inspiration has come from the people and principles I hold dear. My mother, Maria, stands as my greatest source of strength. Her unwavering faith, resilience, and determination carried our family through some of the most challenging times. When we first arrived in Boston, her quiet courage turned desperation into hope. I still marvel at her bravery the day she walked into a church filled with strangers to seek help for her children. That act of faith provided us with food and shelter and taught me that even in the bleakest moments, hope can be found if we dare to ask for it. Her resolve to move forward, no matter the obstacles, remains a guiding light in my life.

Mentorship has also been a cornerstone of my journey. I've been fortunate to encounter individuals who believed in me when I struggled to believe in myself. I think of the neighbor who encouraged my mother to keep me in school after I became pregnant, convincing her that my education was worth fighting for. I think of the professor at UMass Amherst who saw beyond my exhaustion and advocacy work to recognize my potential as a leader. And I think of the community members and colleagues who trusted me to lead, to organize, and to create programs that would serve others. Each of these mentors saw something I couldn't always see in myself, and their belief gave me the courage to persevere. I encourage you to practice the art of mentorship.

I also draw immense inspiration from the communities I've had the privilege to serve. Whether it was the women at Centro las Americas, who showed incredible resilience as they rebuilt their lives through education and advocacy, or the young people I worked with at UMass Medical School, who dared to dream of careers in medicine despite systemic barriers, their stories are a constant reminder of why this work matters. I am inspired by their courage, grit, and willingness to fight for a better future—not just for themselves but their families and communities.

When times were particularly tough, I found solace and strength in believing my work was part of something larger than myself. During my time with Congressman McGovern, I often reflected on the idea of service—what it means to truly serve others, to fight for policies and programs that uplift communities, and to use whatever platform I had to amplify voices that were too often silenced. Seeing the tangible results of our work, from policy changes to individual success stories, reaffirmed my commitment to justice and equity.

Finally, I am inspired by the legacy of those who came before me. I think of the Puerto Rican women in Worcester who fought tirelessly for bilingual education, paving the way for future generations. I think of my *Abuelo*, Pedro, whose love for the land and his family created the foundation on which I now stand. And I think of countless others—activists, educators, and dreamers—whose sacrifices and struggles have made it possible for me to be where I am today. Their stories remind me that I am part of a continuum, a thread in a much larger tapestry of resilience and resistance.

Inspiration, for me, is a remarkable feeling. It allows me to conquer the important tasks that I believe need to be accomplished. It is found in the people who lift us, the communities that surround us, and the belief that our work, however small it may seem, has the power to create lasting change. It is what drives me to keep going, to keep fighting, and to keep dreaming of a better world.

THE ADVICE

If I could share one message with readers, it would be this: *You belong at the table.*

For too long, women, people of color, and the marginalized have been told that they do not have a place in leadership, in decision-making, in power.

That narrative is false. You have every right to be there, but you must also prepare yourself for the challenges that come with claiming that space. Educate yourself, build your skills, and seek out mentors and allies who will support you.

I also encourage you to find your passion—whether it's education, activism, or public service—and pursue it relentlessly. The work of creating change is not easy, but it is profoundly rewarding. And when the door to opportunity is closed, knock it down. Your voice matters.

Lastly, remember the power of community. Surround yourself with people who uplift you, share your values, and are willing to fight alongside you. Together, we are stronger.

THE PATH FORWARD

As I reflect on my journey, I am proud, but I am far from complacent, and I am done. Retirement marked the end of one chapter, but it is not the end of my story. I continue to advocate for systemic change, mentor the next generation of leaders, and fight for a more just and equitable society.

My legacy, I hope, will be one of empowerment. I want young women, especially those from diverse backgrounds, to see my story and know that they too can use their power to move ahead. I want them to know that their dreams, education, and a commitment to justice and themselves can overcome even the most daunting obstacles.

My call to action for readers is this: *Speak truth to power!*

Your voice is needed in your community, your workplace, or the halls of power. Fight for justice, lift others as you climb, and never stop believing in the possibility of a better world.

The path forward is not mine alone—it is ours. Together, we can shape a future where justice, equity, and opportunity are not the exceptions but the norms.

ABOUT GLADYS

Gladys Rodriguez-Parker is a distinguished leader and trailblazer in both government and community service. In 1996, she made history as the first Puerto Rican woman to be appointed District Director for United States Representative James P. McGovern (MA-03), overseeing the Congressman's operations in Massachusetts. Her role involved managing the Massachusetts office, acting as a liaison between the district and Washington, collaborating with local officials, and providing exceptional constituent services.

As a pioneer, Gladys opened doors for Latinos in politics, education, and civic engagement, dedicating much of her time to voter registration and education in marginalized communities. On Election Day, she actively worked to bring voters to the polls, especially in areas where civic engagement was low. She played a vital role in helping candidates at the local, state, and national levels, and was elected as a national delegate in the 2000 and 2004 presidential elections. She also served as one of four Massachusetts Co-Chairs for the Elect John Kerry for President campaign, traveling across the country to support him. Gladys will never forget then Senator Barack Obama's speech. She was in front of the stage and could literally feel the floor from underneath me. That night she knew she saw a future President up close and personal.

One of her proudest achievements is her involvement in the Latino Education Institute, which she co-founded at Worcester State University. This institute helps Latino students and their families succeed in education. Additionally, Gladys partnered with Frank Carroll to secure a permanent home for the Puerto Rico 65th Infantry known as the Borinqueneers at the Central MA Korean War Memorial in Worcester, recognizing the contributions of Puerto Rican soldiers who distinguished themselves in the Korean war.

When Hurricane Maria devastated Puerto Rico, Gladys quickly mobilized efforts in Worcester to support displaced individuals, organizing events and providing assistance to those who sought refuge in the city.

During the COVID-19 pandemic, she worked with local organizations and officials to ensure the safety and well-being of the community, becoming a key figure in the Worcester Working Together initiative.

Gladys is also known for her powerful public speaking skills, using her voice to advocate for important causes and continue her service to others. She has been honored with numerous awards, including:

- AXX100 honoree for 2024 by Amplify Latinx for her work in government and public service
- Commonwealth of Massachusetts State Senate and House of Representatives Official Citations
- United In Purpose Award by United Way of Central Massachusetts for her leadership during the COVID-19 pandemic
- Adelante Worcester Founding Member Award
- Worcester Latino Dollars for Scholars Vision Award
- Ella Poderosa Leadership Honoree Award
- The Key to the City of Worcester, presented by Mayor Joseph M. Petty
- The Barbara Jordan Civic Engagement Award
- Gift of Life New England, Incorporated, Rotary Central Massachusetts Award
- Worcester County Sheriff's Office Official Citation
- Worcester State University Alumni Award

In her free time, Gladys enjoys reading, photography, spending time with family and friends, and traveling. She continues to serve as a powerful voice for her community, with service as her guiding principle.

Learn more and connect with Gladys at:
Facebook @Gladys Rodriguez
Threads/Instagram: @grodparker

GLORIA RIVERA

"I don't negotiate my peace."

\-   Gloria Rivera

~ ~ ~

Gloria Rivera, originally from Baní, Dominican Republic, is a resilient entrepreneur, community advocate, and beauty industry leader. After immigrating to the U.S. in 1994, she overcame language barriers and financial struggles to establish Gloria's Beauty Center in Allston, MA, in 2007. Passionate about empowering others, she became a licensed cosmetology instructor and successfully advocated for a Spanish-language licensing exam for Latina hairdressers. Her community work, including housing advocacy and volunteering, has earned her recognition from Boston officials and organizations. In 2024, she received the Dominicanísimo Award and the City of Boston Legacy Business Award, honoring her dedication to business and community impact.

~ ~ ~

To my children: you have been my inspiration and motivation, driving me to strive for better and do my best. This chapter is dedicated to you

BEAUTIFUL MEMORIES

THE JOURNEY

I am from Bani, a city in the Dominican Republic nestled in the coastal lowlands, just three miles from the Caribbean Sea. My educational journey began there, taking me through middle and high school. Raised by my grandmother and my mom and sister, my cousin greatly influenced me. She was a friendly and responsible person who took the initiative to organize school events. Inspired by her, I began volunteering and getting involved at school, discovering a deep sense of fulfillment and joy in contributing to my community.

My grandmother always stressed the importance of education, often saying, "When you're poor, education is the key to success." She also taught me to trust the process and always remain grateful. Her wisdom instilled a mindset that has shaped my journey.

A pivotal moment in high school came when a teacher recognized my leadership potential and encouraged me to embrace it, sparking a desire to lead and inspire others. This experience was transformative, helping me discover my passion for supporting others. I realized that seeing others succeed brought me immense satisfaction and joy. In high school, I loved socializing with everyone and never felt intimidated speaking to anyone. Whenever students needed to raise funds for prom or other school activities, they often turned to me, recognizing my ability to connect with people and gain their support.

University posed financial challenges; I had to travel two hours to attend and lacked funds for transportation and materials. It was then I discovered my talent for hairdressing. I started doing hair to support myself, turning my living room into a beauty salon. Doing hair helped me pay for everything; it was a skill that helped support my grandmother and me. While attending university, I discovered how different Bani and the capital Santo Domingo were, and I saw that there were more possibilities and opportunities to grow than Bani. Seeing the difference motivated me. Because I was studying communications, I had the chance to visit TV stations, and I enjoyed it immensely.

During a vacation, my mother invited me to Bonaire, where I saw new opportunities. I traveled back and forth before eventually staying there, continuing my hairdressing work. In Bonaire, I met my ex-husband and had my first child. Language barriers and financial struggles made life tough, but I persevered, opening a salon in my house and thriving despite the challenges.

In 1992, my mother passed away, and my ex-husband helped me get a visa to move to the United States. A friend from my hometown in DR let me stay with her, teaching me everything I needed to survive in a new country. Despite language barriers, I adapted, found affordable housing, and got a job.

I moved to the United States because, like many others from Bani, I was drawn by the promise of opportunities—easier access to education, job prospects, and a chance for growth. Boston, in particular, had become a popular destination for people from my hometown. From the moment I arrived, I fell in love with the city. I was captivated by how clean everything was, the exceptional customer service, the sense of discipline, and, most importantly, the safety it provided.

At first, moving to the U.S. was challenging, especially with a three-year-old child and the added stress of not having a Social Security number. Without it, filling out paperwork became difficult and often frustrating. However, volunteering played a significant role in helping me adapt and grow. It made it easier for me to navigate documentation and introduced me to organizations that supported people in similar situations, providing the resources needed to settle into a new environment. The transition felt natural because I came from an open-minded country, and I was never afraid to ask for help or engage with others when I arrived here.

Even after 30 years in the US, I still remember my friend's advice: "Take the job with tips." I learned English, got a car, and became involved in my community by volunteering at the Martha Eliot Health Center in Jamaica

Plain. This volunteer work helped me understand American culture and navigate the challenges of maintaining my cultural identity while integrating into a new society.

In 2006, I went to a beauty school in downtown Boston called Blaine School, where I got my hairdresser license. In 2007, I opened my current business Gloria's Beauty Center located in Allston, MA, in 2008 City Life/Vida Urbana at Martha Eliot Health Center in Jamaica Plain I volunteered to help low-income people obtain housing. While volunteering, I received recognition from Thomas M. Meninio, the Lula Organization, and Dominican Development Center. In 2012, I got my cosmetology instructor license and prepared Latina hairdressers around the city for the cosmetology exam and I also advocated for the City of Boston to have a Spanish version of the test with the help of Albina Lordes and former MA State Senator Anthony D. Galluccio. In Feburary 2023 I received recognition by City Councilor At-Large Julia Mejia for helping small business, personal care, and industries during Covid-19 pandemic. In October 11 2023 I received a recognition by the City of Boston, Pilar de la Hispanidad 2023 Award for the town Allston/Brighton given by current city Concilor of Allston/Brighton Liz Breadon. And, in August 2024, I received the Emprendedora Dominicanisima 2024, an award that recognizes the work and success of Dominicans worldwide. Showing the world the industriousness of their people. I recently received a City of Boston Legacy Business Award for being a small business that has been running for 10+ years, which was awarded by Boston Mayor Michelle Wu.

Each step in my journey, from learning a new language to building a thriving business and advocating for my community, has been a testament to resilience, perseverance, and growth. These experiences have defined my professional path and shaped me into the person I am today—dedicated, community-focused, and proud of my heritage.

THE LEARNINGS

Learning the language was one of my most significant struggles when I arrived in the United States in the 90s. Everything was in English, and it was incredibly challenging to navigate school, where I had to read, write, and learn in a foreign language. Additionally, obtaining a social security number and other necessary documentation added to the complexity of adapting to my new environment.

I learned from those who came before me, gaining insight and inspiration from their experiences. I sometimes felt frustrated, but reading Wayne W. Dyer's *Your Erroneous Zones* helped me understand the importance of setting short-term and long-term goals. This understanding allowed me to clarify my mind, focus on what I needed to do, and enjoy the journey.

Instead of preoccupying myself with unattainable thoughts, I concentrated on the solutions. I understood what I needed would come in time if I continued to

> *Instead of preoccupying myself with unattainable thoughts, I concentrated on the solutions.*

work hard and stay focused. This mindset shift was pivotal in overcoming the obstacles I faced.

In addition to my strategies, I had a support system that was crucial to my journey. Friends and community members provided guidance, helping me navigate the complexities of adapting to a new country. Their support was invaluable, reinforcing my belief in the power of community and connection.

There were times when I challenged established norms and systems. As a Latina immigrant, I disrupted the status quo by pursuing my education, setting up my own business, and creating opportunities for myself and others in my community. This journey, marked by resilience and determination, has shaped me into the person I am today, always focusing on solutions rather than problems. When I created my business, I wanted to make a multicultural place, engaging people from different backgrounds to connect and share stories and experiences with each other.

THE INSPIRATION

My children have always been my greatest inspiration. I wanted to be the best person I could be, believing that if I were good, my children would be good too. This motivation drove me when I came to the United States, pushing me to learn English and understand American culture despite its vast differences from Dominican culture. I wanted to support and appreciate my children as they grew up in an American environment, striving for them to have a better life and succeed on their own paths. Watching them grow and pursue their journeys inspired me to grow as well. Their achievements and resilience have continuously fueled my passion and reinforced my belief that *sí se puede*—yes, you can.

Books like Joel Osteen's "Every Day Is Friday," Robert T. Kiyosaki's "Padre Rico Padre Pobre," Donald Trump's " The Best Real Estate Advice I Ever Received," John C. Maxwell's "The 21 Irrefutable Laws of Leadership" and remarkable women like Princess Diana and Mother Teresa also inspired me. These resources helped me gain a deeper understanding of the bigger picture and opened my eyes to approaching different situations with a level of awareness I previously lacked.

When facing difficult times, I have always thanked God for everything and focused on positive outcomes instead of negative ones. This mindset helped me learn from tough situations and grow stronger.

THE ADVICE

Today, I am passionate about working with others and helping them improve their lives, finding great satisfaction in making a positive impact. Through my business, I meet people from diverse cultures and backgrounds, learn from their experiences, and find inspiration in how they tackle challenges.

> *Don't be afraid to study what excites you, and find a job that brings you happiness so it doesn't feel like work.*

If I could advise my younger self, I would say: don't worry so much about everything. Follow your passions and pursue what you enjoy. Don't be afraid to study what excites you, and find a job that brings you happiness so it doesn't feel like work. Live your life, travel, and get to know different people and cultures. These experiences will enrich your life and help you grow.

I'd advise others on a similar journey to focus on your passions and what truly inspires you. Find work that fulfills you and makes you happy. Make connections with people from various walks of life and learn from them. Embrace the diversity of experiences.

Before having kids, take the time to explore and enjoy life. These moments will build a strong foundation for your future and help you become the best version of yourself.

THE PATH FORWARD

I am a person of faith, always surrounded by positive people who uplift and inspire. I aim to motivate readers to see life as a journey where each step matters. Understanding your goals and remembering that everyone's path is unique is important. Embrace the process, learn something new every day, and savor each moment—what holds significance today may change tomorrow.

In joining this book, I aim to inspire other women to reach their "impossible" goals because nothing is truly impossible. I want to share my journey as a Latina immigrant who came to the United States 30 years ago. From sleepless nights to navigating documentation challenges, I have lived through struggles and triumphs. Building a reliable community, no matter the size, has been a source of invaluable support for me.

Helping others brings fulfillment, and surrounding yourself with positive individuals is essential. But it's also crucial to prioritize your well-being—if you are not at your best, you cannot fully support those around you. I want you to know that "sí se puede"—yes, you can. Enjoy the process, for today's priorities may not be tomorrow's, and embrace every step as part of your unique journey.

ABOUT GLORIA

Gloria Rivera was born and raised in Baní, Dominican Republic, where she was deeply influenced by her grandmother's belief in education as the key to success. Inspired by her cousin's leadership, she became actively involved in school events and discovered a passion for community engagement. Despite financial struggles, she pursued a university education while supporting herself through hairdressing, turning her living room into a salon. Her experiences in Santo Domingo broadened her perspective on opportunities, and during a visit to Bonaire, she found new possibilities, eventually relocating there, where she built a life, started a family, and continued her work as a hairdresser.

In 1992, Gloria immigrated to the United States, seeking better opportunities in Boston, a city known for its strong Dominican community. Despite challenges such as language barriers and financial instability, she persevered, securing housing, learning English, and immersing herself in volunteer work at the Martha Eliot Health Center. In 2006, she obtained her hairdresser's license from Blaine Beauty School and, a year later, opened Gloria's Beauty Center in Allston, MA. Passionate about supporting others, she earned a cosmetology instructor license in 2012 and successfully advocated for a Spanish-language licensing exam for Latina hairdressers with the help of community leaders.

Gloria's dedication to advocacy and business has earned her significant recognition. In 1994, she worked with City Life/Vida Urbana to support low-income individuals in securing housing, receiving commendations from Boston Mayor Thomas M. Menino and community organizations. Her contributions to the beauty industry and Latino empowerment were honored in August 2024 with the Dominicanísimo Award, celebrating Dominican excellence worldwide. Additionally, Boston Mayor Michelle Wu presented her with the City of Boston Legacy Business Award for running a successful small business for over a decade. Through resilience and determination, Gloria has built a thriving career while making a lasting impact on her community.

Learn more and connect with Gloria at:
www.linkedin.com/in/gloria-rivera-21767b155/
https://gloriasbeautycenter.com/

HEIDI M. ROMER

"Everything I need is already within me."

- Heidi M. Romer

~ ~ ~

Heidi Monika Romer is a visionary leader and strategist with 15+ years of experience bridging the nonprofit and private sectors. She specializes in driving impact through collaboration, innovation, and bold leadership.

As an author and speaker, Heidi shares insights on leadership, social impact, and personal growth, helping organizations and individuals create meaningful change. Her entrepreneurial journey is rooted in empowering diverse communities, particularly Latina professionals, through advocacy, policy, and workforce development.

*She has led large-scale community revitalization projects, consulted on national talent strategies, and shaped programs addressing economic mobility and social determinants of health. Recognized with numerous leadership awards, including the **ATHENA Leadership Award Finalist (2022)** and **United Latinas 2023 Amplifying Voices Honoree**, she currently serves on the **UNITED LATINAS Board** and has advised multiple organizations.*

Now focusing on national talent strategy and consulting, Heidi helps organizations build strong leadership pipelines, foster inclusion, and drive meaningful impact.

~ ~ ~

To Every Reader, may these pages inspire you, strengthen you, and uplift your spirit.

To the Extraordinary Latinas authors who dared to bare their souls and become part of history—may we be the spark that ignites change and inspires generations to come.

For my mother, Hilda Luz Santos and grandmother, Waltraute Irmgard Romer - this is for you.

For Barkim, my partner, my best friend, and my greatest supporter.

For my sons, my most profound inspiration.

RISING FROM WITHIN: EMBRACING HERITAGE, OVERCOMING STRUGGLES, & INSPIRING CHANGE

THE JOURNEY

My mother is Puerto Rican, and my father is German. Neither of them was born on the U.S. mainland, but they crossed paths as young adults in Brooklyn, New York—a vibrant hub where cultures collide, diversity thrives, and people from all walks of life come together.

I grew up navigating two distinctly different cultures and belief systems, spending my entire childhood split between the culturally vibrant cities of Miami, Florida, and the Bronx, New York. I loved it. It was what I knew: people, culture, and community.

I am sad to admit I speak very little Spanish and even less German. My mother would tell me she wanted me to speak proper English. I knew there was a lot of meaning behind her comment. I don't take it lightly—living in a time where I can fully embrace myself as a first-generation American, bicultural woman, and proud Latina.

Writing this chapter has given me a newfound appreciation for my upbringing. For the first time, I've genuinely reflected on my childhood through a lens of gratitude. I realize now that my mother and father did the best they could with what they had—and I choose to believe that, not just for them, but for my own peace.

My grandmother had a profound influence on my life. Sitting down around her was not an option, and looking bored was out of the question. There was always work to be done, things to accomplish, and something to learn. And slouching? Absolutely not. I have excellent posture thanks to her—if I ever slouched, she'd come up behind me and give me a firm nudge on the back. She was the best teacher—truly one of a kind. I loved her so much.

I remember everything she told me and tried to teach me. I recall when I refused to eat the crust on the bread, saying it was too hard. She looked at me very seriously and said, "There is no such thing as hard bread; having no bread is hard."

She would always say things like that to me, and it wasn't until I got older that I realized just how much wisdom she had been passing on to me over the years. Her words, simple yet profound, have stayed with me:

Don't tell me how much you make; tell me how much you save. You aren't Princess Diana.

You can't get full off an empty gold plate. Don't focus on shiny things.

Take care of your feet and your teeth. You will always need both.

Dream and do. Because in America anything is possible.

I've always been a dreamer and started many conversations with *"Can you imagine?"* In hindsight, I've always imagined something better for myself and those around me. And that might be why I have always strived for more and have always been a fierce supporter of those around me. I want us all to win. It could also be the influences of my mother and grandmother. *We are who we are because they were who they were. - Maya Angelou*

I'm still a dreamer. It's taken my lifetime, but my dreams are becoming a reality. I'm the inaugural Managing Director at Work Renewed, a Black-owned and women-led national talent strategy and consulting firm. I can now say I am an author, which has been a huge dream of mine for a long time. I'm also a speaker, and now that I've rediscovered my voice, I plan to explore the possibilities in this space even more. And I am excited to share that I am an entrepreneur. I am the founder of H.O.L.A. Books, an online book store specializing in Latino authors. I have so many plans. I'm leaning into this business wholeheartedly, and I know the universe will help me. If you're wondering, H.O.L.A. stands for Heidi's Only Latino Authors.

My cultural identities, the places I've lived, the people in my life, my experiences, my triumphs, and tragedies all shaped my life. I wish they were here to see that I made it, I'm making it, and I will always make it. I believe the way you show your family you love them is how you choose to live your life.

I choose to be my fiercest advocate and support and uplift others.

I choose to be resistant and not accept things as they are for myself and my community.

I choose to be fearless in pursuing the life I want, just like my family did when they came to the U.S.

I choose to be the person who wants to help as many people as I can.

I don't want people to struggle and have to live through the hardships I've experienced. My life's work has been and continues to be in a people-first and community-centered space.

THE LEARNINGS

I've faced many challenges throughout my life, starting as early as twelve years old. That was a pivotal year in my life and the first of many years of struggle and hardship for me. Poverty robs you of so much, but you can't let it strip you of all the good that's inside you—your heart, your spirit, and your mind.

There is power in the way you talk to yourself. My survival-driven mantra was *you can't beat me*. This applied to everyone and everything. I said this to myself for a long time. Years later, and after much reflection and growth, I realized my mantra was about refusing to let my spirit be broken. I still feel this way, but I now have a more nurturing mantra: *everything I need is already within me*. These few words remind me to embrace who I am just as I am. This mantra helps ground me and hypes me up.

When you are forced to depend on yourself, you learn to navigate the world differently. I had to choose whether I would fall or fly, and I chose to fly— no matter what it took to make it happen.

As a teenage mom, I graduated high school six months early. It took me ten years to complete my bachelor's degree, but I never gave up and successfully achieved it. I don't remember ever thinking about how hard things were at the moment. I focused more on my dreams and doing whatever it took to push through. For example, when I went to my high school counselor to ask what I needed to do to graduate early in January. And as he tried to make it seem impossible, all I could think about was how I refused to have it any other way. I had no idea how difficult it would be to navigate through college. Everything was a challenge and cost money I didn't always have at the time – applying to college, registering for classes, figuring out financial aid, and most importantly finding a reliable babysitter. It wasn't easy. I put myself through college, and I graduated much later than I had planned. I never gave up. Thank you to all the teachers who allowed me to bring my two sons to class so I wouldn't miss a lesson or a test.

I survived years of mental and physical abuse from the age of 17 to 23. One moment turned into many moments. One time spiraled into a hundred times. And one day turned into years. What should have been the best years of my life were some of the worst. I had two little boys that depended on me. I was so young and alone. I felt completely lost. I was embarrassed and broken. My spirit was shattered. It took me a very long time to start living again and loving again.

I have to thank my sons. There was a moment when I thought to myself "You are all they have, the one parent, the one person in their life, so you better be the best parent you can be. And no one will love them the way you do, so get it together and make it happen." That was a turning point in my life.

My sons and I were homeless for a long time. It's still hard for me to talk about it. If I talk about it, I'll have to think about it, and if I have to think about it, then I'll have to deal with all the emotions that come with it. And those emotions can be like wild horses - uncontrollable. During that particular time in our lives, my biggest concern was that no matter what happened, we were together and would always be together - and we were. Thank you to everyone who offered help, a kind word, a hot meal, and a place to sleep.

Now that my life is different, these acts of kindness look different, too. It's connection, collaboration, exposure, and growth. Thank you to everyone who says my name in a room full of opportunities. I'm on my way.

There were many acts of kindness, powerful conversations, and life changing moments along the way. I am thankful for those who have come into my life for only a season and a lifetime.

I never gave up on myself, *and* I kept dreaming about the life I wanted to live *and* I wanted to break generational curses *and* I kept going for my sons and myself *and* I refused to accept things as they are *and* I became my biggest advocate and advocate for those around me *and* I stopped being afraid *and* I embraced who I am deeply.

Keep dreaming, keep learning, and keep going. Refuse to have it any other way.

THE INSPIRATION

Inspiration can be found in so many places and forms. It can come from the people around us and from within, from our dreams, goals, and desires. The beauty is that it's everywhere, waiting to be noticed and embraced.

When I was young, I remember being around people I didn't want to be like. I'm thankful for those experiences. That was the beginning of aspiring to be more.

I remember the stories my grandmother shared with me about her life. She was ahead of her time in so many ways. That inspired me to fight for what I want. My mother was beautiful and dressed beautifully. She was my first teacher and influencer. She inspired me to be mindful of how I show up and present myself.

I lived in between the Bronx and Miami for most of my life – from city life to beach life and back again. There was always so much to see and do and be part of. I have always loved being a part of communities, different cultures, diverse people, and eating international food - I'm a foodie. That's all I knew. I'm Puerto Rican and German, my best friend was Vietnamese, my babysitter was Italian, I attended Catholic church on one side, Lutheran on the other side, and my neighbors practiced Santeria. This was my life, and I'm glad I was exposed to so much living. These experiences helped inspire me to always be curious, to learn from others, and embrace all cultures and my cultures fully.

As my life changed, it was a natural progression for my reasons of inspiration to evolve, too. I've been running from poverty and chasing freedom for a long time. I aspire to never live in poverty again. Doing the best I can in trying to help those around me is also a source of inspiration. And my ultimate source of inspiration are my sons.

I am also an avid reader and believe in the power of words in all forms. One of my favorite books is *The Alchemist* by Paulo Coelho. I love all of the messages, especially about how when you truly want something, the universe will help you achieve it.

THE ADVICE

Looking back at my teenage years in particular, I would tell my younger self to be strong and stand firm in your beliefs. There will be moments when you feel lonely, when fear seems overwhelming, but everything

It may feel like it will bever ger better. But it does. And you will rise, and you will make it.

you need to overcome already lies within you. The journey ahead won't be easy, and it may feel like it will never get better. But it does. And you will rise, and you will make it.

I would say to be selective of who you allow into your world. To protect your peace, that's non-negotiable. It's essential to do what's best for you. I would share the airplane example of putting your oxygen mask on first before helping others too. I would tell my younger self that when you finish high school, it's not the end of anything, but the beginning of everything. You are beautiful and unique, and there isn't anyone in the galaxy like you. To embrace who you are deeply. To follow your dreams and never give up.

I wish I had someone to tell me these things when I was younger. However, I don't know if I would have listened. I thought I was so tough and understood everything. All 5 feet 3 inches of myself.

From the most challenging moments in my life, I learned a valuable lesson on how to not stay stuck in the mire. When *you can't beat me,* wasn't enough, I learned to *put a limit on your pain.* Feel what you need to feel and reclaim your power to move forward. And don't think you have to do it alone; we all need our community. And you get to define what community means to you - friends, family, co-workers. It's o.k. to reach out and accept kindness and support.

I strive to be the person I wish I'd had in my life—especially for other women. I would encourage women to do the same. To lead with love and kindness. Remember your past circumstances don't define you. Never allow anyone to have the power to change who you are or your character. You don't have to accept things as they are. Never shrink for anyone. Look straight ahead, hold your head up high with your shoulders back, and walk into every room like God sent you.

Everything you need is already within you. You are the author of your own story.

I believe in the power of words, especially self-talk. You need to make sure you aren't your own harshest critic, and you are being kind to yourself. Be your own hype woman. You are still standing, and you aren't going anywhere. You are a strong Latina woman. No one can beat you. Everything you need is already within you. You are the author of your own story. Remember that.

THE PATH FORWARD

This book is a dream come true for me—a reminder that the time to act is now. It's not just my story, it's our stories, our moments, and the beauty of our collective unity. I hope my story inspires you to be fearless in your pursuit of the life you want to live. To have the courage to imagine something better for yourself.

Latina women do not have the luxury of being undecided. Know what you want and go after it.

Be your own fiercest advocate. Because if not you, then who?

As you rise, reach back, link arms, pull up, and push forward those around you - especially women.

ABOUT HEIDI

Heidi Monika Romer is a visionary leader, connector, and advocate for transformational change. With over 15 years of experience bridging the nonprofit and private sectors, she has built a reputation as a dynamic strategist who drives impact through collaboration, innovation, and bold leadership.

As an **author and speaker**, Heidi shares insights on personal evolution, leadership, and social impact—helping organizations and individuals create meaningful change. She is a sought-after thought leader known for her ability to see the big picture while navigating complex systems with precision and purpose.

Her **entrepreneurial journey** is rooted in a deep commitment to empowering communities, businesses, and individuals. From leading large-scale community revitalization projects to consulting on national talent strategies, Heidi's work has spanned hyper-local grassroots initiatives to national-level transformations.

A **first-generation American and bicultural leader**, she has been a champion for diverse communities, particularly Latina women and professionals, ensuring they have the tools, resources, and networks to thrive. Throughout her career, she has played a pivotal role in shaping policies and programs that address social determinants of health, workforce development, and economic mobility.

Heidi has been recognized with numerous **leadership awards & nominations**, including:

- **2022 ATHENA Leadership Award Finalist** – Honoring women leaders making a profound impact

- **EPIC Robert L. Wilson Award for Exceptional Service & Leadership**

- **Certificate of Recognition from the Mayor of Buffalo, NY** for her leadership in the refugee and New American community

- **United Latinas 2023 Amplifying Voices Honoree**

She currently serves on the **UNITED LATINAS Board**, a global organization dedicated to amplifying the voices of Latina professionals and fostering leadership development. Previously, she served on multiple **boards and advisory committees** throughout Western New York focusing on children and families, community health, food justice and women's advancement.

Now focusing on **national talent strategy and consulting**, Heidi helps organizations build strong leadership pipelines, develop impactful community engagement strategies, and create workplace cultures that foster inclusion and innovation.

Her journey—from community advocate to business leader—demonstrates her ability to **bridge worlds, break barriers, and build legacies**.

Learn more and connect with Heidi at:
Website: www.heidimonika.com
LinkedIn: https://www.linkedin.com/in/heidimonika/
Coming Soon H.O.L.A Books, LLC

ISABEL ARGOTI

"Never let anyone put out your fire without your consent. Fuel your spirit, understand the power of your flame, and spread love through your warmth."

\-   Isabel Argoti

~ ~ ~

.Isabel Argoti, a proud first-generation Ecuadorian-American, is passionate about empowering youth, supporting first-generation students, and advocating for women and girls in Montgomery County, Maryland. She has held impactful roles at the National Park Service and Collegiate Directions, where she led key initiatives, and has demonstrated strong leadership through community programs such as LADYS-CVILLE and the Hispanic College Institute. Isabel served for five years on the Montgomery County Commission for Women, chairing notable committees and leading the 44th Women's Legislative Briefing. Recognized with several awards, including the Presidential Lifetime Achievement Award in 2024, Isabel is currently the Deputy Director at Community Bridges, a board member for AMP Global Youth, and Vice President of FlanCake by Gaby. She holds a B.S. in Architecture from the University of Virginia and a Nonprofit Management Executive Certificate from Georgetown University.

~ ~ ~

To the beloved women who poured into me and raised me:
mis abuelitas, tias, hermanas, y mi mami.
Ustedes llenan mi corazón.

A LATINA'S LIGHT: EL PODER DE ENCONTRAR TU CONFIANZA Y COMUNIDAD

THE JOURNEY

I was born in a small town nestled between mountains, a volcano, and waterfalls. My hometown, Baños de Agua Santa in Ecuador, is just as magical as it sounds. My first home is the heart of my beautiful family. My grandparents, parents, tías, and tíos all settled their lives here for us hijos y primos to thrive with humble businesses, community connections, and stories to share for a lifetime.

My parents decided to immigrate to the United States when I was just shy of 2 years old. My father came first to scout new opportunities and potential work. Soon, my mom joined him, and later, my older sister, Gaby, and I were sent to reunite with our parents after about a year. I've been told that I had to be lulled to sleep to make the flight calmly—a sign that even at my youngest, I did not want to part ways with my familia and beautiful Baños.

I've also been told that I forgot who my father was and no longer recognized him once I came to the States. It saddened me to learn this because I could not imagine my life without my father. My tías and primas took care of me in Ecuador before it was safe to send my sister and I. This hard time apart at such an early time in my life serves as a reminder that my family members will forever support me, my parents, and we stick together. The sacrifices of our parents are limitless, and I'm forever grateful to them for going to extraordinary lengths—not just leaving their families behind, but bringing us along to build a better life.

We lived in Washington, DC, for a few years. My earliest memories flash back to 16th Street in a yellow apartment building. My parents, sister, uncles, and I made it work. We had a two-bedroom apartment. I can still picture the street view from the window because I remember that we sometimes had to throw the mice out the window.

Later, we moved up to Wheaton, Maryland—just north of Washington, DC—and this was a huge help for our education. Montgomery County Public Schools is a much better school district than Washington, DC. I now realize how much my zip code made a difference in the trajectory of my education. I ended up in gifted and talented programs with access to after-school programs, athletics, and advanced courses. While still not perfect, I realized I had opportunities and unlocked doors.

But still at times, it felt like I was juggling two different friend groups and personas: the "studious" classroom friends and the "cool" friends outside the classroom. My classmates in my AP courses were extremely smart and affluent, and they often did things together after school. I didn't always feel like I could belong and resorted to being on the shyer end. I got my work done and was friendly with all, but it didn't feel like mi gente.

I also had friends outside of my advanced courses—those I ate lunch with, danced alongside on the Latin dance team Titanes Salseros, and whose parents trusted mine, allowing us to hang out at each other's houses after school. These friends looked like me and I could relate to them because we had immigrant households, shared similar foods at home, and had parents who could speak Spanish to each other, giving us all a sense of connection and understanding.

I sometimes felt like I had to balance two worlds. I loved both, but I didn't think I could combine them. I didn't feel like I could truly be both. Years later, I realized this was my way of learning to "code switch" and navigate my identity. This idea of belonging, feeling seen, and finding validation in who you are in different spaces.

Experiencing this world as a young woman, immigrant, and Latina can be daunting. I have many "firsts" that I continue to figure out, but instead of living in fear, I found a way to create excitement for these firsts through my curiosity and creativity. I started trying new things alone, signing up for events, and putting myself in new spaces to push my comfort zone little by little.

These experiences pushed me to be confident in the duality of my identities –the quirky things I proudly like doing, and my unique cultura that I will always hold close to. This mosaic of aquí y de allá makes the beauty of my life today. And I love to share it. I am often the one to attend a community event and invite a friend. Or travel to somewhere new and bring my family along to see the world. Or volunteer for a committee to grow in leadership while advocating for my community. I'm still learning more about myself each day, and in this process, I'm finding ways to ignite my identity. To truly love her, por mi misma. Reflecting back on my journey from my time in my little Ecuadorian pueblo to now in top leadership roles building a future for my family and community, I have to remind myself –guao, what a beautiful ride indeed.

THE LEARNINGS

Growing up, I joined swim teams following my dad's encouragement. He saw it as a noble sport that "American girls" did. My dad has always been my biggest cheerleader. He is a true girl dad who instilled in the three of us the importance of education and good character. His extroverted and resilient nature helps him connect with practically everyone, and I admire how he never lets himself be defeated.

While I enjoyed swimming, I often felt out of place. Usually, I was the only Latina on my team. Sometimes there was an Asian girl, which brought some comfort, but usually, I was the only girl of color. I noticed other differences as well. Other girls arrived in private school uniforms with expensive shampoos, while I had a basic gym bag and was picked up in my dad's work truck. Plus, no one taught me how to treat my curly hair after chlorine-filled practices. I cycled through bottles of conditioner, hoping to tame the frizz. It seemed as though I shared a pool and locker room with my team, but not much else.

It wasn't until I joined my summer team, Glenmont Gators, with swimmers from all backgrounds, that I finally felt, "Wow, this is fun, and I belong here." Swimming is a uniquely vulnerable sport, where you compete individually and are exposed in nothing but a swimsuit. But through swimming, I gained so much self-esteem and body confidence, and as a Latina, this was huge. For me, it became both physical and emotional therapy, helping me embrace myself amid society's unreasonable expectations.

Swimming was a constant through difficult times. When my older sister Gaby was diagnosed with a brain tumor, my family's life shifted completely. It was scary. Our days became long as we commuted daily to Baltimore where she was hospitalized for about a year. My dad did his best to ensure I still attended swim practice so I could have a sense of normalcy. Still, I often completed homework at the hospital or played with my sister Natalia in the hallway, as she was too young to enter the room. I became very independent, aiming to do well in school to lighten my parents' load as they navigated the healthcare system, language barriers, and their own emotional struggles. I believe I matured much earlier than most, driven by necessity, and developed a profound appreciation for life. I'm happy to say that Gaby has fully recovered since then, has started her passion projects, and she continues to be one of my biggest role models.

A few years later, a huge blessing arrived when my family and I became U.S. citizens. Qué orgullo. During the swearing-in ceremony, I distinctly remember a government official correcting me on my full name. He emphasized with noticeable disdain,: Isabel Geovanna Argoti Barrionuevo. Throughout my school years, I had simply been registered as Isabel Argoti, so I never realized my full name included both my father's and mother's last names. This newfound understanding of my name ignited a deeper curiosity about my roots. To honor this realization, I prioritized having my full name proudly printed on my college diploma—an enduring tribute to my heritage, ancestors, and family. And ensuring no one would ever repeat my name in such disrespect.

Becoming a citizen transformed my education. I qualified for federal aid, and with support from Collegiate Directions Inc. (CDI), a first-generation college access program, I attended college debt-free. My years of dedication were paying off. Still, I felt the need to prove myself. During my 12th-grade year, my English teacher collected data about scholarships. I proudly wrote $60,000 per year at the University of Virginia. Just writing that big of a number was scary—I'd never known that kind of money, and somehow it was mine. When my teacher collected my sheet, he paused and asked, "Isabel, this is yours?" Yes. Mine. His surprise was a reminder of the barriers I was breaking as a Latina with a full ride to a top public university. It was my motivation to keep surprising people.

I attended the University of Virginia on a full ride and graduated from the School of Architecture. Being an architecture major was no easy feat and our classmates lovingly called us the "zombies' because we were known for getting no sleep and designing all night. My inspiration for architecture came from my dad who worked in construction my entire life. I was amazed each time I witnessed a new home that was managed and built by my father's hands. Studying architecture was a beautiful mix of my love for art, skills in math, and what I was familiar with at home. In an ideal world, I would enter a family business designing projects for my father to make a reality. It was also a secure future and tangible job that I could explain to my family.

However, in my third year, I realized I had a stronger love for culture, community, and youth. I had opportunities to study abroad in many countries, join and start clubs, volunteer in a juvenile detention center, and mentor local youth. This opened my eyes to the world beyond my little corner and problems I could solve with my expertise. While I decided it was too late and strenuous to change my major, I took electives in education, youth innovation, and volunteered for community programs where I put my skills to use.

After graduation, I completed an internship with the National Park Service in Denver, Colorado. I was a Communications & Urban Outreach Intern, combining my interests beautifully —my expertise with the built environment, understanding of underserved communities, and creativity for design and communication. This unique experience through the Latino Heritage Internship Program allowed me to create incredible connections and learn of really neat projects. I also realized that there were jobs beyond the "traditional". I shifted my focus to community outreach.

I eventually managed the national Every Kid in Park Program in the U.S. Department of Interior right after the change in administration in 2016 and made it my duty to keep programs like this alive for our future generations – even in my limited capacity. After my fellowship, I wanted to continue to make an impact in my local community. I had skills to share and I wanted to lift others up, especially students. I returned to the same beloved organization that helped me enter college, CDI, and only moved up from there. Incredible mentors pushed me to apply for manager positions and complete a post-grad certification program at Georgetown University.

Before I knew it, I was a leader dedicated to public and community service. I'm not sure if I necessarily knew nonprofit management as a career path at the age of 18, let alone a job for which I could earn a salary, but here it was. Recently, I was humbled to receive the Presidential Lifetime Achievement Award from the White House for my years of volunteer and civil service. In my career, I completed two AmeriCorps services, a fellowship year, and years of local community projects totaling well over 4,000 service hours. My family actually surprised me with this award, reminding me that my passions started with the learnings and teachings at home –a full circle moment.

I am now going on 10 years into my profession, and I love how it's all been a unique recipe for my skills and passions. I'm finding my purpose. As I progressed in my journey, I realized my degree did not define me. Sometimes we restrict ourselves to the decisions we made as just a teen, without giving ourselves permission to adapt, change, and embrace. Architecture gave me an incredible design background and unquestionable work ethic for what I do today in nonprofit management but it was my lived experiences, the new experiences I leaped into, and my community that mattered the most for my success. Sure, there were plenty of times when I was the youngest in meetings, the only woman, or the "newbie," but having a seat at the table was significant.

THE INSPIRATION

My inspiration comes from the incredible women in my life. I am deeply proud and honored to be surrounded by strong women, and they have fueled my work with women, girls, and the Latino community. This includes my work at Community Bridges, empowering girls in Montgomery County, my involvement with the Commission for Women, and my sorority.

One of my most significant sources of inspiration is my younger sister, Natalia. She was born when I was in sixth grade, and I remember proudly telling my friends about her. The eleven-year age gap between us adds a unique dimension to our bond. She is the first U.S.-born person in our family, and while she may not realize it, she plays a huge role in my life. Being her role model has given me profound motivation, pushing me forward even in tough times.

The matriarchs in my family have also shaped who I am. As I grew older, I learned about the resilience of the women on my mother's side: entrepreneurial spirits who held our culture and traditions close. I learned how my late Tia Lourdes took care of me as a baby while my mom made the difficult journey to cross the border. I learned how my Tia Margarita and Tia Piedad went to Italy in search of a better life, and soon my Tia Margarita returned to Ecuador to take over the family restaurant. She even started using her gift to give back and feed the poor in poverty neighborhoods. Philanthropy and comunidad runs in my blood.

And my dear mother, though quieter about her struggles, has always been a guiding light. She works diligently at every task, bringing our home to life with seasonal decorations, preparing traditional foods, and instilling values that keep our culture alive. She preserves our culture and uplifts our family. I hope to one day become even a fraction of the remarkable woman she is.

My mother always supported my dreams. She eagerly joined me on college visits, viewing it as a world of new possibilities she had never experienced herself. I was the first in my family to move away for college and felt both excitement and guilt as I left home. I was the only one from my friend group to leave for college, and no one from my high school attended the University of Virginia. I was stepping into the unknown, but I trusted the guidance of those trusted adults who told me to go for it.

College was a new experience, but I quickly noticed the stark contrast between my background and that of many wealthy legacy students with long ties to the University. Many students had inherited views about race and class that didn't align with my experience. I joined Latino groups but still felt a gap. My peer mentor invited me to learn about a Latina sorority, and my head tilted— a Latina what? I was introduced to Sigma Lambda Upsilon/Senoritas Latinas Unidas Sorority, Incorporated (SLU). I learned about its mission to empower Latinas and promote literacy. I finally met other Latina women who attended college, graduated, had masters degrees and PhDs, and continued onto incredible professional roles while uplifting their culture, families, and giving back to the community. I was sold.

In 2013, four of us founded the Alpha Rho Chapter at University of Virginia. Our chapter has now flourished to over 40 Hermanas, and we continue to uphold our sisterhood across the nation. Seeing what the Alpha Rho Chapter has grown to now and seeing young girls in college, once like me, finding their community in us, keeps me going. It's a constant reminder that my actions and leadership can influence future generations. It's a reminder that when people feel your intentions are genuine, they'll join you, and together, you can make a lasting impact.

When people feel your intentions are genuine, they'll join you, and together, you can make a lasting impact.

THE ADVICE

I continue to learn about myself as I enter new phases of my life. While I would give my younger self advice, I wouldn't necessarily change anything about my experiences. I'm a strong believer that things happen for a reason. Whether good or bad, situations are handed to you because you are strong enough to handle them. God has a reason and a purpose for all experiences. Trusting the process is sometimes the biggest test of patience.

I would tell the younger me to let go of doubt and what others think of me. I tended to hold back, even when I knew I was more than capable. I was fearful of being made fun of, not fitting in, or not doing the "right" thing. I wanted to be accepted but didn't realize that being my best self would be the best thing I could offer the world. I would eventually find and share my talents with the world, but it took some time. I hope young girls today know how much they are valued, loved, and embraced for their uniqueness. There is no one else like you. I make it a point to remind the girls I interact with of this truth, ensuring the magic of their unique talents is amplified and shared.

> *I believe that you should lead everything with love. Love the world more, love others, and do what you do with love.*

I believe that you should lead everything with love. Love the world more, love others, and do what you do with love. While choosing to love is important, I advise being thoughtful and selective about who you extend your kindness to and how you do so. Something I forgot to do along the way was to love myself. Unable to prioritize my self-love led me to compromise my self-respect and value. You are the protector of your peace and should not let yourself be taken advantage of. I have been a victim of dating violence where I mistook manipulation and abuse for attention and love. I thought the repeated patterns of toxic attention meant I had to work harder to be "loved" and keep giving my kindness without conditions.

Trust your gut. If something doesn't sit right with you, trust that feeling and say something. A woman's instinct is unmatched, and it's one of our best superpowers. Learn to listen to it and trust it because good things come with time. I am now happily in the healthiest relationship with a partner that respects and honors me.

Lastly, I advise you to help one another, especially as sisters. The idea that we are in competition with each other or in constant comparison is old and ugly. Let go of this mindset. Be a good friend to your fellow girlfriends. Check up on each other, catch up over dinner, buy each other flowers, laugh with each other, share your struggles, hold each other during the hard moments, and empower each other. We are each other's greatest treasure as we navigate this world.

THE PATH FORWARD

I hope you move through this world like the queen that you are, filled with all your special gifts, talents, and magic that you offer—the magic that is already within. I ask that we be kind to one another. I ask that we extend a helping hand to gracefully guide and uplift one another, especially when the climb feels like a shaky ladder reaching too high.

We owe it to our ancestors and ourselves to make an effort to preserve our cultural traditions, teachings, and stories. In a world that sometimes feels too busy, I hope you find the time to slow down, love, empower, and embrace. These deep soul connections, stories, and values are what will truly be passed on once you remove the busyness of fame, fortune, and technology.

I hope to make a meaningful difference in my corner of the world. Just as my beautiful Baños de Agua Santa is such a small treasure with a beautiful influence, I hope to continue to use bits of my talents and compassion to uplift those around me. My greatest aspiration is to inspire others—especially the next generation—to embrace their confidence, pursue their dreams, and know they are never alone in their journey. Juntas, we can build a stronger, more connected comunidad where every story matters and every voice is heard for generations to come.

ABOUT ISABEL

Isabel Argoti is a first-generation professional with proud roots from Ecuador. Isabel holds a strong passion for developing youth programs, helping first-generation students, advocating for women and girls, and continuing her local involvement in Montgomery County, Maryland, where she grew up.

Professionally, Isabel worked at the National Park Service and U.S. Department of Interior managing the Every Kid in a Park program. At Collegiate Directions, she established the Career Mentoring Initiative. She credits much of her leadership to her community involvements including helping form the LADYS-CVILLE mentorship program, serving as a team LEAD for the Hispanic College Institute, and her various roles at Sigma Lambda Upsilon/Senoritas Latinas Unidas (SLU) Sorority Inc. Isabel also served on the Montgomery County Commission for Women for 5 years where she served as Vice Chair, chaired Emerging Leaders and Public Relations committees, and led the 44th Women's Legislative Briefing — the longest standing women's conference in Maryland.

Isabel has humbly received the Presidential Lifetime Achievement Award from the Office of the U. S. President in 2024, the Baila4Life 2024 Trawick Inspiration Award as an alum of her latin dance team, and the 2022 Rising Star Award from the Montgomery County Business and Professional Women.

Currently, Isabel is the Deputy Director at Community Bridges where she manages program strategy to empower girls throughout the county in grades 4-12. She is a Board Member for AMP Global Youth and newly formed nonprofit for the Wheaton Arts & Entertainment District. She is also the Vice President for FlanCake by Gaby, a family-run business bringing joy and community through delicious flancake dessert. Isabel also works on several creative design and marketing projects for clients.

Isabel graduated from the University of Virginia with a B.S. in Architecture and earned her Nonprofit Management Executive Certificate from

Georgetown University. She loves a good coffee, likes to crochet, and enjoys spending time with her family and friends.

Learn more and connect with Isabel at:
Linkedin: https://www.linkedin.com/in/iargoti/
Website: http://bit.ly./m/iargoti/

JACQUELINE GERENA

"My sazón is rooted in compassion, relatability, and a genuine approach that not only builds trust but leaves a lasting impact."

\-   Jacqueline Gerena

~ ~ ~

Jacqueline Gerena is a recognized thought leader in pharmaceutical risk management, leading a team at a prominent pharmaceutical company to develop and implement innovative strategies that ensure patient safety, regulatory compliance, and access to life-saving therapies. She is deeply committed to advancing equitable healthcare and empowering the next generation of leaders. As a Board Member of Women of Color in Pharma (WOCIP), Jacqueline co-leads the Next Generation Pillar, creating opportunities for mentorship and professional growth in the life sciences. A sought-after speaker at pharmaceutical and women's empowerment conferences, she is widely respected for her insights and strategic vision. Jacqueline holds an MBA from Post University and a bachelor's degree in Criminology from Central Connecticut State University. Residing in Connecticut, she enjoys traveling, advocacy work, and spending time with her family.

~ ~ ~

To my family, whose unwavering love and support have been the bedrock of my journey. Especially my parents, Pedro and Candida Gerena, who instilled in me the values that have shaped every step of my path; and my daughters, Taina and Isabella, who light up my life and remind me daily that the future is boundless, brilliant, and waiting for their radiance to illuminate it. To every dreamer who dares to reach for the moon—this chapter is for you. May it inspire you to embrace your uniqueness, overcome every challenge with grace, and believe in the extraordinary mark you are destined to leave on the world. Dream boldly. Rise unapologetically. Shine endlessly

RISE BOLDLY, LIVE FIERCELY: A LEGACY OF EMPOWERMENT AND PROGRESS

THE JOURNEY

Becoming the changemaker I am today is a testament to resilience, determination, and pivotal moments of challenge and triumph. As the youngest of three children in a close-knit Puerto Rican family, I learned early on that leadership wasn't a title but an action. I grew up translating at doctor's appointments, navigating complex systems for relatives, and stepping into responsibilities well beyond my years. These early experiences planted the seeds for the leader I would one day become.

I am a proud first-generation American, raised in a home where Puerto Rican culture was at the heart of everything. My parents were deeply rooted in their heritage and passed that pride on to me and my siblings. Growing up, our identity wasn't just something we celebrated—it was woven into every part of our lives, from the food we shared to the values we held dear. My father, a laborer who worked his way up to foreman, taught us the importance of self-reliance, often reminding us, "As long as you can get up and work, you will get up and work. The day you cannot, you go with your head held high and ask for what you've paid into." My mother, with her unwavering generosity and big heart, showed me the power of service, always reminding us that "adonde come uno, comen dos" (where one eats, two can eat).

Their example shaped my worldview and instilled in me a sense of pride and responsibility that I carry to this day. In our family, being Puerto Rican wasn't just a label—it was a way of life. It meant standing tall in the face of adversity, finding strength in community, and lifting others as we climbed. Even now, my family and I take every opportunity to celebrate and share our culture, because it's not just where we come from—it's who we are.

Growing up in New Britain, an inner city in Connecticut's Hartford County, came with its challenges. As a child, I witnessed and survived situations no child should face. From being approached by gangs as a third grader to surviving a drive-by shooting in fifth grade, my environment tested my resolve. Yet, my parents' example gave me the tools to rise above these circumstances and dream beyond the boundaries of our reality.

One of the most defining moments in my life came at 19 when I became a mother. What others saw as a limitation became my greatest motivation. I balanced full-time work, an 18-credit course load in college, and the responsibilities of raising my daughter, Taina. I embraced intentional networking, sought mentors and sponsors, and built a career development plan that aligned with my vision for the future. These deliberate actions ensured that my circumstances didn't dictate my trajectory. Instead, they became the fuel for my aspirations.

These formative experiences laid the foundation for my career. While my undergraduate degree in Criminology reflected a desire to address systemic inequities, my transition into the pharmaceutical industry 15 years ago opened doors I hadn't envisioned. I entered a field where women of color are underrepresented and have built a career navigating unspoken challenges and breaking barriers. Throughout this journey, I've relied on mentors, sponsors, and an unshakable commitment to excellence.

Today, as I pursue a doctorate and reflect on my path, my purpose remains clear: to inspire and uplift others. My daughters, Taina and Isabella, remind me daily why I work tirelessly—not just for their futures but for those who look to me as an example.

My story proves that where you start does not define where you can go. Your determination shapes your future, your choices, and the support network you build along the way. I embrace every step of this journey with passion and purpose, knowing it has prepared me to be the changemaker I was destined to be.

THE LEARNINGS

The most pivotal challenges I've faced stem from being underestimated—both as a woman of color and a non-clinician in a highly specialized field.

Despite my accomplishments, I've repeatedly had to prove my expertise and combat doubts about my capabilities. Early in my career, leaders questioned my ability to lead programs due to a lack of clinical credentials. Despite successfully managing these initiatives, I often confronted bias and microaggressions.

When new leadership doubted my expertise and reassigned my responsibilities, I leaned into my knowledge and negotiated terms that reflected my value when they sought my return. I learned to approach challenges strategically, turning doubts into opportunities to demonstrate resilience and capability.

Every obstacle became an opportunity to grow. I equipped myself with knowledge, always prepared with accurate information and a clear understanding of the topic at hand. I embraced curiosity, knowing that asking questions was a strength, not a weakness. Initially, I navigated these challenges alone, as my family, though loving and supportive, had no experience in corporate America or the pharmaceutical industry. Their belief in hard work and quiet perseverance—keeping your head down and waiting for recognition—was a mindset I had to unlearn. Breaking free from that approach was transformative, allowing me to thrive in a competitive and ever-evolving field.

When my company announced a relocation to Boston, I knew immediately that moving wasn't an option for my family. My youngest daughter had recently been diagnosed with a rare immune deficiency that required life-saving infusions every three weeks, and my eldest daughter was finally thriving in a school where I had fought hard to secure the accommodations she needed. Uprooting them simply wasn't on the table.

At the same time, I couldn't afford to lose my job—our health insurance was critical. I decided to take a bold step and negotiate for what I deserved. My work in pharmaceutical risk management was highly specialized, and I understood the value I brought to the company. While the fear of losing everything loomed over me, I stood my ground and played my cards strategically. Ultimately, the gamble paid off, and I secured a role that allowed me to stay in Connecticut, protect my family's stability, and finally be compensated fairly for my expertise.

Looking back, that experience taught me the immense power of self-advocacy and the importance of knowing my worth. For too long, I had been content with being undervalued, thinking that simply having a job was enough. But this situation made me realize that advocating for myself wasn't just about me—it was about setting an example for my daughters, ensuring their future, and proving that women, especially women of color, deserve to be at the table and compensated accordingly. It was a defining moment that reaffirmed my belief in standing firm, even when the stakes feel impossibly high.

That situation also highlighted the importance of negotiation. For years, I hesitated to advocate for myself, believing I should simply be grateful for my achievements. But a pivotal moment—learning that my replacement would be hired at a significantly higher level and salary—served as a wake-up call. I began approaching opportunities differently, negotiating terms that reflected my worth and securing positions aligned with my long-term goals. Negotiation is not just about compensation; it's about recognizing and advocating for your value.

THE INSPIRATION

My family has been my most significant source of inspiration, especially during challenging times. My parents, the foundation of my strength, came to this country with no formal education but unwavering determination. My father fulfilled his promise that my mother would never have to work, becoming a pillar for our family and teaching me the power of hard work and integrity. My mother, though illiterate, is the wisest and most resourceful person I know, embodying leadership through character and action. Growing up in a tough neighborhood, I witnessed my parents treat everyone with dignity and kindness, even those society feared, instilling in me the importance of empathy—a principle that shapes my personal and professional life.

When times were tough, my family motivated me to keep going. As a teenage mother, I faced doubt and criticism, but instead of letting it hold me back, I used it as fuel to prove I could succeed. I felt a profound responsibility to fulfill my parents' aspirations for me, honor their sacrifices, and uphold the legacy of our family name. My success became a personal goal and a way to inspire future generations and show that perseverance triumphs over adversity.

My inspirations have grown to include trailblazing Puerto Rican women who have shattered barriers, like Supreme Court Justice Sonia Sotomayor, the first Latina on the Supreme Court, and Dr. Antonia Novello, the first female and Hispanic U.S. Surgeon General. Their dedication to equity and public service exemplifies what's possible when representation and determination converge. Meeting Dr. Novello recently was an honor, and her pioneering leadership and commitment to healthcare equity deeply inspired me.

Joining Women of Color in Pharma (WOCIP) provided me with a community that celebrated authenticity and ambition. WOCIP became my extended family, offering mentorship, encouragement, and tools to navigate my career confidently and purposefully. Their emphasis on equity and representation aligns with my passion for creating opportunities for others, especially those from underrepresented backgrounds.

My daughters have profoundly strengthened my sense of purpose. My eldest, with her remarkable resilience in facing mental health challenges, inspires others through her journey and reminds me daily of the importance of self-awareness and advocacy—values that resonate deeply in our family, especially after the loss of my brother at just 34, a devastating reminder of the critical need for mental health care and support. My younger daughter, our "rainbow baby," is a testament to perseverance. Despite living with a rare medical condition, navigating a recent autism diagnosis, and facing social adversity, she has blossomed into a strong, determined young lady whose resilience inspires me every single day and reinforces the strength we all possess.

Every success I achieve is a tribute to the struggles of those who came before me and a commitment to honor their dreams, uphold our family's name, and inspire the next generation.

THE ADVICE

If I could offer advice to my younger self, it would be this: Always bring your authentic self into every space you enter. Embrace the richness of your cultural heritage and the unique perspectives it brings—not as obstacles but as invaluable assets. Your authenticity is your power and will set you apart in ways you cannot yet imagine.

Looking back, I wish I had realized the vast career opportunities in STEM sooner. Math and science came effortlessly to me—I took extra courses in high school and earned top grades in college statistics and biology while balancing work and motherhood. Yet, my vision of career possibilities was limited to the roles I saw around me: teachers, nurses, and doctors. Representation matters deeply. Had I been exposed to the life sciences industry earlier, I would have known the opportunities were as boundless as my potential.

For anyone navigating a similar journey, know this: you are not limited by others' perceptions of you. Never let skepticism or doubt diminish your ambitions. I faced these challenges, too, but with the unwavering support of my family and the resilience forged as a young mother, I surpassed expectations, proving that success knows no bounds.

As you navigate your path, identifying individuals who can serve as mentors and sponsors is critical to your growth, development, and career trajectory. I call them my "personal board of directors." These people provide guidance, open doors, and challenge you to reach higher. Remember, as your journey evolves and you reach new levels, your board of directors should adjust. The insights and support you need at one stage may be different from what's required at the next.

Additionally, a habit that has been instrumental to my growth is asking myself, when presented with a new opportunity—personal or professional—what I will gain or learn from it to grow and prepare for the next step. This mindset has served me well. Professionally, I've always excelled in my current roles by proving my capabilities through action and raising my hand for ad hoc projects that further stretched me. I evaluate every role through the lens of what skills and knowledge I will acquire to make me more marketable in the future.

It's equally important to invest in your growth and development. While many organizations offer development programs, these are often limited in availability, may not incorporate the realities faced by Latinas and women of color in the workplace, or fail to align with the individual career goals we set for ourselves. Waiting for someone else to prioritize your growth can leave you underprepared or dissatisfied. Instead, consider your personal and professional development as a standard financial investment in your future, much like any other key priority in life. Whether pursuing a certification, engaging a career coach, or attending conferences and workshops, these investments will yield substantial returns—enriching your skill set, building your confidence, and positioning you to navigate and shape your career on your terms.

As the demands of my career have increased, I've also had to learn to set boundaries—a skill that has required continuous work with the help of a career coach and therapist. These boundaries have been vital for maintaining a sustainable balance between career growth and personal well-being. Time boundaries ensure I dedicate specific hours for work, take scheduled breaks, and reserve non-negotiable personal time for family and self-care. Workload boundaries help me say no to excessive tasks, delegate effectively, and prioritize career opportunities aligned with my values. Health boundaries allow me to focus on wellness, normalize taking mental health days, and prevent burnout. These practices have been essential in fostering long-term success and personal fulfillment.

Seek spaces that celebrate your uniqueness. The world is increasingly recognizing that diversity fuels innovation, and your voice—shaped by your experiences—is critical to this progress. If one door doesn't open, find another, or build your own.

Remember, the journey is about personal achievement and paving the way for those who come after you. Your courage and determination will inspire others—whether it's your children or other young people watching you persevere—to believe in their limitless potential.

> *No challenge is insurmountable; assess, plan, and don't hesitate to ask for support.*

The habits that have fueled my growth are rooted in embracing challenges with strategy, resilience, and collaboration. No challenge is insurmountable; assess, plan, and don't hesitate to ask for support. As the saying goes, "If you want to go fast, go alone. If you want to go far, go together." Growth isn't a race—it's a deliberate journey of becoming better today than you were yesterday. With patience and focus, you'll lay a foundation for success that lasts a lifetime.

Carry your cultural heritage with pride and let it fuel your ambition. Every step you take forward creates a path for others to follow. Together, we can transform what is possible for ourselves and future generations.

THE PATH FORWARD

The legacy I hope to inspire through my story is one of resilience, empowerment, and collective progress. As a proud descendant of strong, determined women, I am raising two daughters to carry this legacy forward. I am deeply aware that my actions are more than personal—they reflect my family, my culture, and the global community of women of color striving to break barriers and redefine what is possible. This responsibility is both humbling and empowering, and I embrace it wholeheartedly. I stand on the shoulders of my ancestors, who sacrificed and dreamed so that I could have opportunities they never could.

My journey is not just about personal achievement but about honoring their sacrifices by uplifting others, creating a ripple effect of progress that touches everyone around me. For me, success is not an individual pursuit but a shared victory, a collective triumph that strengthens our communities.

To others, my message is clear: lift as you climb. As you rise, bring others with you. Leadership is not about titles or positions; it's about service, compassion, and the courage to create spaces where others can thrive. Recognize the humanity in every individual, value their unique contributions, and amplify the voices that too often go unheard.

> *Leadership is not about titles or positions; it's about service, compassion, and the courage to create spaces where others can thrive.*

True leadership is building bridges, not walls; it is planting seeds of change for a future that includes everyone. Reflect on the legacy you want to leave behind. Let it be one of hope, action, and transformation. Take pride in your heritage, your story, and your voice—these are your greatest assets. Use them to challenge the status quo, disrupt outdated systems, and demand a more equitable and inclusive world.

Your story has power. Your presence matters. Your actions create change.

Born to Puerto Rican parents and shaped by the rich fusion of Taino, Spanish, and African traditions, my cultural identity is the foundation of who I am and how I lead. These traditions have instilled in me a sense of empathy, emotional intelligence, and an unwavering commitment to service. In my professional and personal endeavors, I strive to embody the values of community, reciprocity, and collective well-being that define Puerto Rican culture.

Leadership, for me, is not about climbing to the top alone—it's about building a ladder strong enough to carry others with me. Through my journey, I aim to inspire others—especially women of color in STEM and beyond—to see their limitless potential and embrace their heritage as a source of strength.

I want my daughters, my nieces, and generations of young girls to know they can dream boldly, break barriers, and lead authentically. We are not here to fit into molds but to shatter them and create new paths.

Let us honor those who came before us by becoming the catalysts for the change they envisioned. Let us demand equity, celebrate diversity, and build a future where success is not the exception but the expectation. Together, we can create a legacy of resilience, empowerment, and hope—a legacy that will inspire the world to dream bigger and do better.

ABOUT JACQUELINE

Jacqueline Gerena is a distinguished thought leader in pharmaceutical risk management, serving at a prominent pharmaceutical company. She leads a risk management strategy team dedicated to designing, developing, implementing, and continuously optimizing required risk management programs across multiple therapeutic areas. With a focus on mitigating risks to patients, her work navigates the complexities of regulatory requirements and risk management standards. Her team collaborates closely and negotiates with the FDA to ensure compliance while adapting to evolving regulatory expectations. Under her leadership, the team plays a critical role in upholding patient safety, advancing public health, while minimizing undue burden on the healthcare system. Their efforts reflect a steadfast commitment to ensuring the safe use of medicines and maintaining patient access to life-saving and life-transforming therapies.

Jacqueline's unwavering dedication to making an impact is evident in every facet of her work, from advocating for equitable healthcare to fostering mentorship and representation for women and people of color. As a Board Member of Women of Color in Pharma (WOCIP), she co-leads the Next Generation Pillar, focusing on empowering and cultivating future leaders in the life sciences industry. One of her signature achievements is the development and execution of the WOCIP Virtual Career Connections Micro-Conference, a groundbreaking platform designed to connect college students of color with opportunities and insights into the pharmaceutical and life sciences sectors. Through this initiative, Jacqueline creates spaces for learning, mentorship, and networking, reflecting her deep commitment to advancing diversity, equity, and inclusion. By nurturing the next generation of talent, she is helping to ensure that the life sciences field reflects the diversity of the communities it serves.

Beyond her role at WOCIP, Jacqueline's work extends to the broader professional community. As an Advisory Board Member of the RISE Women's Leadership Conference, she actively supports initiatives that inspire and empower women across industries. Previously, she served as an Advisory Board Member for the University of California, Irvine Division of

Continuing Education, where she contributed her strategic expertise to support lifelong learning initiatives. Her commitment to mentorship and leadership underscores her passion for creating opportunities for women to thrive and succeed.

Jacqueline's professional career is equally impressive. Previously, she served as Director of REMS Programs at Aimmune Therapeutics, a Nestlé Health Science company, where her strategic leadership drove the success of global and U.S. risk management programs, earning her the prestigious Pinnacle Award from the Aimmune Executive Leadership Team. Her career is further distinguished by impactful roles at Titan Pharmaceuticals, Alexion Pharmaceuticals, and Aetna, where she consistently delivered results and demonstrated her commitment to operational and strategic excellence.

Jacqueline Gerena is a recognized thought leader and sought-after speaker, frequently invited to share her expertise at pharmaceutical and women's empowerment conferences. Her engaging insights and strategic vision have earned her a reputation as a catalyst for meaningful progress and innovation in the industry. Jacqueline's expertise has also been featured in pharmaceutical industry publications, further underscoring her influence, and thought leadership.

Her academic achievements reflect her dedication to excellence and lifelong learning. She holds an MBA from Post University and a bachelor's degree in Criminology from Central Connecticut State University. Further demonstrating her commitment to advancing her knowledge and leadership capabilities, she has commenced work toward earning a doctorate.

Residing in Connecticut with her husband, Jose, and their daughters, Taina and Isabella, Jacqueline balances her professional pursuits with a deep appreciation for family and community. An avid traveler and advocate, she finds joy in exploring new cultures, championing important causes, and creating lasting memories with her loved ones.

Learn more and connect with Jacqueline at:
Linkedin: www.linkedin.com/in/jgerena123

JEANETTE VELASQUEZ

"ASK…Keep Asking, Keep Seeking, & Keep Knocking."

-   Jeanette Velasquez

~ ~ ~

Jeanette Velasquez is a dedicated wife, mother of four, grandmother, and the visionary founder of Velasquez Tax & Business Services LLC (VTBS) and Core Values Strong Families Inc., a nonprofit organization. With a deep passion for empowering communities, Jeanette focuses on providing resources that enhance lives spiritually, financially, educationally, and technologically.

~ ~ ~

This chapter is dedicated to my late mother, my cherished grandmother, and the remarkable Sophia Simmons—women whose love, sacrifices, and enduring wisdom continue to guide and inspire me daily. Their legacy is a reminder of the power of faith, resilience, and unconditional love. I also dedicate this work to the underdogs, the castaways, the overlooked, and the underestimated—the ones who have been chosen last, counted out, or tirelessly working in the shadows without recognition. To you, I say: Remember, you carry the oil. You hold the strength, resilience, and divine purpose needed to illuminate even the darkest paths. Your efforts are not in vain, your value is immeasurable, and your moment to shine is nearer than you think. Keep pressing forward—you were made for greatness.

KEEP ASKING, KEEP SEEKING, KEEP KNOCKING: A LEGACY OF TRANSFORMATION

THE JOURNEY

In 1982, my life began under circumstances that could have easily defined me as a statistic—a child conceived as the result of rape, with dark skin, bifocals, and a fragile sense of self-esteem. At just five months old, I was placed in foster care due to my biological mother's struggle with postpartum depression and eventual addiction, a casualty of the devastating "War on Drugs" that gripped our community. Yet, amidst this uncertainty, I was divinely placed in the care of a selfless, loving woman who would transform the trajectory of my life.

She became the only mother I've ever known—a woman who later brought my biological sister into her home straight from Boston City Hospital. Together, we grew up in a house filled with life: a grandmother I adored, a rotating cast of foster children, and an extended family from all walks of life. It was a home that embodied resilience, love, and the power of community.

My grandmother's unwavering affirmation of my worth stood in stark contrast to the negative comments I endured from neighborhood kids and even some family members who ridiculed my complexion and features. She told me I was beautiful, intelligent, and capable. Her love laid my growth foundation, while her practical teachings planted the seeds for my life's purpose.

I vividly remember walking to her home on Northampton Street in Boston, navigating bustling streets and back alleys just to spend time with her. Despite her limited mobility due to a fire in the Orchard Park Projects, she invited me into the kitchen after watching Julia Child on TV. "Baby, you wanna go in the kitchen and fix us a meal?" she'd ask. Joyfully, I would prepare simple meals like spam and sauerkraut, grateful for the opportunity to serve her.

One of the most transformative experiences of my childhood began when my grandmother entrusted me with managing her monthly finances at the age of 10. A man who came to cash her check—someone I later discovered was exploiting her—was the catalyst for me stepping into a role of responsibility. I carefully created a budget for her rent, cable, phone bill, food, and other necessities. My tasks included making grocery lists, walking to Tropical Foods on Washington Street for shopping, cashing checks for money orders to pay her utilities, and cooking her meals.

Though I was just a child, I carried the weight of responsibility and the importance of financial literacy. I didn't realize it then, but those monthly rituals—handling money orders, balancing expenses, and ensuring every dollar was accounted for—were shaping the skills and mindset that guide my career today.

By 14, I transitioned from working for my grandmother to my first official job, but the lessons I learned in her home were profound. They taught me discipline, resourcefulness, and the deep satisfaction that comes from others.

Those early experiences laid the foundation for my passion for financial literacy, my curiosity about finance, and my commitment to empowering others to navigate their financial challenges. Looking back, it's clear that the life I was born into didn't define me; the life I chose to build did.

My mother's and grandmother's unwavering faith in me—their belief in my abilities even when I couldn't yet see them myself—has been the driving force behind my journey as a changemaker and financial advocate today.

THE LEARNINGS

As a teenager searching for love and identity, I fell into the arms of a man I thought would fill the void of not having a father figure. He was older, handsome, and captivating—a Black Puerto Rican man I believed was my world. But in reality, I was a naïve 9th-10th grader blinded by infatuation. My life revolved around him, and I ignored the wisdom and guidance of my mother, who saw the dangers I couldn't.

My mother's warnings were constant, but I thought I knew better. I disrespected her, stayed out with my boyfriend and friends, and put her through unimaginable pain. Missing over 50 days of my sophomore year, I was on the verge of being a high school dropout. My mom had enough and began the process of filing a Children in Need of Services (CHINS) order against me. Standing in that courthouse, I faced a moment of reckoning. I didn't want to end up in the juvenile system—a place where so many kids who looked like me were trapped. I saw my future for the first time and realized I wanted to be more than another statistic.

The following year, I committed to change. As a junior, I went to school every day, rediscovered my love for math, and found a new passion in accounting. My accounting teacher introduced me to filing taxes, and I vividly remember getting my first refund from a summer job. That simple act—filling out forms and receiving a reward—ignited something in me.

Around the same time, women in my church stepped in as mentors, showing me what stability and success looked like. They took me on trips, shared their lives with me, and modeled a world of possibility. Inspired by their examples, I started attending Bible study, surrounding myself with positive influences, and focusing on my future. I got a summer job at Gillette Headquarters, earning $16 an hour—a huge boost for a 17-year-old. For the first time in years, my life had structure, and I was thinking about college, savings, and becoming the person I wanted to be.

But just as I was getting on track, life threw me another challenge: I discovered I was pregnant. At 17, the fear of telling my mother was overwhelming. When I finally mustered the courage, her disappointment was palpable. But I made a promise to myself and her: I would finish high school, go to college, and raise my child to succeed, no matter what.

Determined to keep that promise, I enrolled in a school for pregnant teens, where my GPA soared. I was named "Most Changed" in my yearbook and applied to several colleges. I worked part-time, saved money, and meticulously planned for my future as a mother and a student.

Even though my child's father was absent—lost to drugs and jail—I was not alone. Despite her initial disappointment, my mother loved her grandbaby,

Chayanne, with all her heart. I also leaned on a supportive community of older adults serious about motherhood. Their guidance, combined with my determination, kept me focused on my goals.

Through this journey, I learned about resilience, the importance of community, and the power of intentionality. Every obstacle became a stepping stone, shaping me into a young woman with a purpose. I discovered that with faith, discipline, and the right support system, I could overcome anything—and I did.

My journey wasn't just about survival; it was about transformation. It was about becoming the person my younger self needed and showing my daughter that no matter the odds, you can rise above.

THE INSPIRATION

In my first year of college, I majored in Accounting and earned an impressive 3.75 GPA. At 18 years old, I managed life as a young mother with my daughter enrolled in a great private preschool and living in my first apartment. During that time, an extraordinary Accounting professor offered me kindness and unwavering support. Being the only young single mother in the class, I often felt isolated, but her encouragement made me feel seen and capable. She even supported my daughter, helping me juggle the challenges of pursuing my associate's degree. During this time, I also volunteered with the Volunteer Income Tax Assistance (VITA) program, providing free tax preparation for low-income and elderly taxpayers. Helping others receive tax refunds and save for the future was an eye-opening and liberating experience that planted the seeds for my passion for financial empowerment.

After completing my associate's degree, I set my sights on earning my bachelor's degree, believing education was the key to success—as my mother and society had always said. But reality hit hard. I was saddled with $30,000 in student loan debt by the time I graduated. I couldn't afford to return to school full-time, and making $12.75 an hour wasn't enough to cover basic expenses in Massachusetts, even with an affordable apartment. Between rent, food, car insurance, my daughter's private preschool, and mounting bills from creditors, anxiety and depression took hold. Despite budgeting, the math didn't add up, and no one around me ever mentioned the concept of increasing cash flow. My daughter and I soon found ourselves homeless.

Homeless, employed, and without a shelter option due to earning "too much" income, I hit rock bottom. Going back to my mother's already overcrowded apartment wasn't an option. It felt like my world had collapsed. Then, I discovered Bridge Over Troubled Waters, a nonprofit that offered counseling, support, and shelter for mothers without income restrictions. This became a turning point. During this season of setbacks, I found the strength for one of the greatest comebacks of my life.

At the shelter, I began to see the cracks in the system—the cycles of emergency assistance programs and lack of financial literacy designed to keep people in poverty. I prayed, "Abba Father, I need a program that will allow me to return to school, put my daughter in a safe space, and help me develop leadership and financial skills."

I didn't stop there. I enrolled in a bachelor's program, applied for housing, and sought every opportunity to improve our circumstances. One day, while riding the bus to my volunteer internship, I overheard two women discussing a program called One Family Scholars. I leaned in and asked, "Did you say this program pays for you to go back to school? Can you tell me more?" They did, and I applied as soon as I reached my stop. To my joy, I was accepted into the program, which covered my schooling, supported my daughter's needs, and provided leadership development.

With the help of One Family Scholars, I moved out of the shelter, completed my bachelor's degree in Accounting with a minor in Entrepreneurship, and found my life's purpose. This journey ignited my passion for advocating for financial literacy, equitable housing, homeownership, and creating opportunities for those who need it most.

What began as a season of despair became a testimony of resilience and purpose. Today, I'm dedicated to breaking barriers and empowering others, ensuring that no one else has to navigate the challenges I faced without the tools to succeed. My story isn't just about survival—it's about thriving, rebuilding, and creating a legacy of empowerment for generations to come.

THE ADVICE

I can genuinely say I have been blessed by looking back over my life and thinking things over. The trials, setbacks, rejections, and challenges were all part of the path that led me to where I am today. Without them, I wouldn't be the fighter, overcomer, and trailblazer that I am—dedicated to my husband, Lionel Velasquez, our four children, and our grandson, and to the many lives I am destined to touch with empowerment and purpose.

If I could offer advice to others, here are the lessons that have shaped my journey:

1. **Embrace Your Setbacks as Setups for Growth.**
   Life is full of unexpected valleys—poverty, homelessness, foster care, heartbreak. Each of these moments feels unbearable, but they hold the seeds of your strength. Use every setback as a learning opportunity. These experiences don't define your destiny; they refine it. For me, the challenges of growing up in foster care and becoming a single mother at 17 weren't the end of my story. They were the foundation for my resilience and my commitment to serve others.

2. **Be Intentional with Your Vision.**
   Success doesn't come by chance; it's the result of purpose and planning. I learned this at 10 years old, managing my grandmother's household budget after her devastating house fire. Those early lessons in financial literacy laid the groundwork for the careers and businesses I've built today. Whether you're managing your personal life or a business, map out your vision and take intentional steps toward it every single day.

3. **Surround Yourself with a Supportive Community.**
   We are not meant to walk this journey alone. Throughout my life, I've been blessed with mentors, church members, and friends who saw my potential. I doubted myself. They taught me that community isn't just about networking; it's about finding people who believe in your vision and hold you accountable. Their encouragement gave me the confidence to pursue higher education, start my businesses, and make an impact in my community.

4. **Lead with Service and Purpose.**

   True success isn't about how much you achieve for yourself but how much you can uplift others. That's why I founded Velasquez Tax & Business Services LLC and Core Values Strong Families Inc. My mission is to provide resources that empower others spiritually, financially, and educationally. From helping small businesses secure over $1 million in pandemic grants to increasing their profitability by 30%, my goal has always been to create ripples of change beyond my immediate circle.

   > *True success isn't about how much you achieve for yourself — it's about how much you can uplift others.*

5. **Faith Is Your Foundation.**

   Through every challenge and triumph, my faith has been my anchor. It has taught me to trust the process, even when I couldn't see the end result. Faith isn't just about belief—it's about action. It's about stepping out into the unknown, knowing that each step is divinely guided.

6. **Always Be a Lifelong Learner.**

   Whether it's learning to file taxes at 17, volunteering with the IRS's VITA program, or adopting new technologies for my clients, I've embraced every opportunity to grow. Growth doesn't stop after school—it's a continuous journey. Equip yourself with knowledge, and don't be afraid to step outside your comfort zone.

In closing, my advice to anyone reading this is simple: Don't let where you start to determine where you'll finish. Whether you're a struggling single parent, a small business owner, or someone trying to find your purpose, know that you can overcome any obstacle with faith, intentionality, and the right community. Your story matters, and your impact can create ripples that transform not just your life but the lives of others.

THE PATH FORWARD

> *Your story is not defined by where you start but by the legacy you choose to build.*

To my fellow Latinas, dreamers, and warriors who face life's challenges with courage and grace—this is my call to you: Rise up. Your story is not defined by where you start but by the legacy you choose to build. My journey has been one of trials and triumphs, and if there's one thing I've learned, it's this: your voice, dreams, and contributions matter.

For too long, we've been told to accept limitations placed on us by circumstance, society, or even our doubts. But I'm here to tell you those limitations are not your reality. You have the power to rewrite your narrative, break barriers, and create opportunities—not just for yourself but for those who come after you.

Throughout my life, I've seen the beauty of resilience and the power of community. I've faced rejection, homelessness, and the weight of systemic inequities, but with every step, I've also witnessed the transformative power of hope, faith, and action. I've gone from being a young single mother struggling to make ends meet to becoming the founder of two impactful organizations. These aren't just achievements—they prove what's possible when we dare to believe in our potential.

So here is my message to you: take action. Whether that means starting a business, pursuing an education, advocating for change, or simply taking the next small step toward your dreams—do it with intention, courage, and the unwavering belief that you are worthy of success. Surround yourself with mentors and community members who will uplift and inspire you. Seek out resources, knowledge, and opportunities, and don't be afraid to ask for help.

And remember, our community thrives when we lift as we climb. Be the one who opens doors for others, plants seeds of hope, and creates a ripple effect of change. Whether you're mentoring a young girl, advocating for policy changes, or simply sharing your story, your impact is immeasurable.

My story is not unique—it is shared by so many Latinas navigating life's challenges with grace and grit. My legacy is to show you that you can rise above any obstacle and create a life filled with purpose and meaning. Together, we can build a legacy of empowerment, excellence, and equity for generations.

I challenge you today to take that first step, no matter how small it may seem. Embrace your story, own your power, and know that you are capable of creating extraordinary change. The world is waiting for the brilliance only you can bring. Let's make it happen—together.

ABOUT JEANETTE

Jeanette Velasquez is a dedicated wife, mother of four, grandmother, and the visionary founder of Velasquez Tax & Business Services LLC (VTBS) and Core Values Strong Families Inc., a nonprofit organization. With a deep passion for empowering communities, Jeanette focuses on providing resources that enhance lives spiritually, financially, educationally, and technologically.

Her entrepreneurial journey is rooted in the inspiration she drew from her late adoptive mother and grandmother, who instilled in her the values of dedication and service. At just 10 years old, Jeanette began managing her disabled grandmother's household budget, which laid the foundation for her unwavering commitment to breaking barriers and helping others access equitable resources.

Despite facing the challenges of growing up in foster care, experiencing poverty and homelessness, and being a single parent, Jeanette became the first in her family to graduate from high school and college. She also dedicated over eight years to volunteering with the IRS's Volunteer Income Tax Assistance (VITA) program, providing free tax preparation services to low-income individuals and families.

Since founding VTBS in 2008, Jeanette has played a pivotal role in the economic empowerment of individuals and organizations across various sectors. Her leadership has facilitated the acquisition of over $1 million in loans and grants for small businesses, especially during the pandemic, demonstrating her commitment to innovation and problem-solving in the financial services sector.

Learn more and connect with Jeanette at:

Website: https://vtbsuccess.com/
Linkedin: https://www.linkedin.com/in/jeanette-velasquez-064524266/
Non-profit: http://cvsfamilies.org/

JEANNIE MARMOL

"Opportunities often arise in unexpected places, and every open door has the potential to lead somewhere transformative"

\-   Jeannie Marmol

~ ~ ~

As CEO and founder of Millionaire Latina, Jeannie cultivates a broad community dedicated to fostering resilience and empowering others to attain lasting financial freedom. Jeannie demystifies finance as part of her mission, making it accessible, inspiring, and actionable for a diverse audience. Her multifaceted approach encompasses personalized one-on-one coaching, corporate consulting, dynamic workshops, and impactful speaking engagements.

~ ~ ~

If you are reading this chapter, then this is for you. You are truly special, and your story is worth telling. Never forget that every experience you go through adds to the tapestry of your journey—one that holds meaning and deserves to be shared.

A special dedication to my mother, for teaching me the true essence of courage and leadership. To my daughter, Arianna, for being the unwavering strength that inspires me to keep going. And to my partner, Delfina, for always encouraging me to take risks and standing by my side through it all

PIVOT, PERSEVERE, PROSPER: LESSONS FROM A LIFE TRANSFORMED

THE JOURNEY

My journey began in Harlem, where my mother and I arrived when I was just five years old. She was only 20 at the time, a teenager when she had me, and we had no home, no family to rely on, and no knowledge of the language. Those early years were unimaginably difficult. We slept on floors, often went without food, and struggled to find a sense of stability. My mother, however, is one of my greatest heroes. She faced every obstacle with grit and determination. Despite being young, uneducated, and alone in a new country, she taught me that persistence is the key to survival, even when the odds are against you.

Eventually, after several years of hardship, we were able to move into a Section 8 apartment. While it provided some stability, the challenges didn't end. My mother worked tirelessly, often 12-hour shifts, for just a few dollars an hour. I grew up quickly, taking on responsibilities far beyond my age. By the time I was eight or nine, I was helping her manage the household bills, deciding which ones we could afford to pay each month. Looking back, I realize how these experiences shaped me—they instilled resilience, resourcefulness, and the understanding that hard work is non-negotiable.

Growing up in Harlem in the 1980s was no small feat. The streets were riddled with drugs, violence, and systemic neglect. Statistically, I wasn't supposed to make it out. Teenage pregnancy, welfare cycles, and hopelessness were expected outcomes for kids in my neighborhood. But I was determined to rewrite that narrative. My mother's mantra was clear: education is the one thing no one can take away from you. I promised her that I would study hard and use my education to create a better life for us.

When I was 13, a teacher saw my potential and introduced me to the A Better Chance program, a scholarship opportunity for underserved students. The odds were slim—thousands of kids vied for one scholarship—but I applied. To my disbelief, I won. That phone call changed my life. However, it meant leaving my home, my community, and my mother to attend a boarding school in Connecticut. I was terrified but determined. I promised my mother that I would come back and make her proud.

Boarding school was a culture shock. I quickly realized how far behind I was academically compared to my peers, and I spent three years catching up. It was one of the hardest experiences of my life, but it taught me resilience, adaptability, and the value of stepping out of my comfort zone. When I graduated, I received a full scholarship to Mount Holyoke College. Walking across the stage with my diploma at 22 was a moment of triumph—not just for me but my family. I kept my promise to my mother.

After college, I thought I would go to medical school, but financial barriers made it impossible. Instead, I accepted a job at JP Morgan Chase. It wasn't part of my plan, but that opportunity opened doors I never imagined. I started as a banker and climbed the ranks over nearly 20 years to become an executive director overseeing $6 billion in assets and 12 branches in Manhattan. For a Latina from Harlem, breaking barriers in corporate America was a milestone I was immensely proud of.

Then the pandemic hit. New York City became Ground Zero for COVID-19, and life as I knew it changed forever. I lost loved ones, including my stepfather and grandmother. My daughter struggled with virtual schooling and mental health, and my health deteriorated without answers from doctors. It was a wake-up call. I realized I needed to make a drastic change—for my daughter, my health, and our future. So, I boldly decided to leave my corporate career and move to Miami.

Miami became a fresh start. It was here, while networking and reflecting on my next steps, that I identified a significant gap: Latinos, particularly women, lacked access to financial literacy and guidance. Inspired by my journey, I founded Millionaire Latina, a company dedicated to coaching and empowering Latinas and their families to redefine wealth on their own terms.

For me, financial freedom isn't one-size-fits-all. Whether it's owning a luxury condo in Manhattan or traveling the world as a digital nomad, it's about aligning your finances with your dreams. My mission with Millionaire Latina is to inspire others to realize that, no matter where you come from or what your circumstances are, you can achieve financial success and live a life of abundance.

Today, I'm helping women and families rebuild their dreams, create generational wealth, and reclaim their narratives. My journey has taught me that resilience, reinvention, and community can transform lives. And now, I'm committed to helping others rewrite their own stories. Together, we're building a legacy of empowerment, excellence, and equity.

THE LEARNINGS

Life has taught me that resilience isn't just about surviving adversity—it's about learning, adapting, and thriving in the face of it. As the first in my family to graduate from college and earn an MBA, I know firsthand the challenges of

Life has taught me that resilience isn't just about surviving adversity – it's about learning, adapting, and thriving in the face of it.

navigating uncharted territory without a roadmap. No one in my family had walked this path before me, so I had to find support, seek guidance, and create strategies to overcome obstacles.

One of the most important lessons I've learned is the power of community. Being the eldest and the first in my family to accomplish many milestones, there was no one to turn to for advice. My mom, though my rock, didn't understand the systems I was navigating. My brothers now look to me for guidance, but who do I turn to? The answer, I discovered, is community.

Community doesn't find you; you have to seek it out. When I moved to Miami, I didn't know a soul. I didn't even know the streets around my new apartment. So, I turned to tools like Meetup to find events and meet people who resonated with my vision and values. I relied on past relationships, like my connection with the CEO of ALPFA, who introduced me to the Miami chapter. These relationships became lifelines, offering support, mentorship, and camaraderie. I learned that leaning on the connections you've built and actively seeking out new ones is essential to growth and success.

Another key lesson is never to close a door. Opportunities often arise in unexpected places, and every open door has the potential to lead somewhere transformative. Moving to Miami was one of the hardest decisions I've ever made. Leaving a six-figure salary, a career where I was respected, and a life of familiarity to start over was terrifying. There were days in that first year when I questioned everything. But deep down, I knew I was being guided by something greater. My gut and faith told me to trust the process, and I did.

Pivoting has also been a recurring theme in my journey. When one path no longer serves you, it's okay—even necessary—to change direction. After almost 20 years at JP Morgan, the pandemic forced me to re-evaluate my life. Losing loved ones, watching my daughter struggle with virtual learning, and facing my health issues made me realize that the life I was living was no longer sustainable. I had to pivot, and in doing so, I found a new purpose with Millionaire Latina.

Through all of these transitions, I've developed coping mechanisms that keep me grounded. Faith and prayer have always been cornerstones of my resilience, providing a sense of stability even in the most uncertain times. Exercise was once my go-to, and while I no longer run five miles a day, I've found solace in other practices. Journaling, particularly gratitude journaling, helps me focus on the positive, even on difficult days.

Meditation has also become vital to my life, but I've learned it doesn't have to look a certain way. For me, it's about quieting my mind through breathing exercises and grounding techniques. Living near the beach has been a blessing; I've discovered that connecting with nature—feeling the sand beneath my feet or the grass against my skin—helps release tension and reset my energy.

Each of these practices, combined with my willingness to adapt, has helped me stay focused and positive, even when faced with immense challenges. They've taught me to lean into uncertainty with faith, to rely on my community, and to pivot when necessary.

> *Your circumstances do not define your future.*

If there's one message I'd like to leave with others, it's this: your circumstances do not define your future. Where you are today doesn't dictate where you'll end up. The setbacks, challenges, and obstacles are not roadblocks but stepping stones. Lean into them, learn from them, and use them as fuel to build the life you deserve. Trust your journey, embrace your community, and never be afraid to pivot when the time comes.

THE INSPIRATION

Inspiration has been the heartbeat of my journey, coming from extraordinary individuals and unexpected moments that have shaped my path. My mom, my greatest role model and hero, is at the center of it all. Her courage to leave everything she knew—her country, her language, and her support system—to build a better life for us in a foreign land is something I carry with me every day. At just 20 years old, she packed her dreams, her grit, and her five-year-old daughter and embarked on a journey with nothing but $20 in her pocket and an unwavering belief that we would find a way.

Now, as a mother myself, I look back in awe of her strength and resilience. Would I have had the courage to do the same? Would I have taken such a leap of faith with so little? My mom's story is a testament to her tenacity and a reminder of what's possible when you have grit and the willingness to take risks. Her example fuels me to push harder, dream bigger, and face challenges with the same resolve she demonstrated daily.

But inspiration doesn't stop there—it has shown up in the form of people I call "angels" who crossed my path at just the right time. The teacher who introduced me to the scholarship program that changed my life is one such angel. She saw something in me that I didn't fully see in myself and gave me the push I needed to dream beyond the confines of my circumstances. Then there were the mentors at JP Morgan who helped me find my footing in the corporate world, guiding me as I navigated uncharted waters as a young Latina woman. Each played a vital role in shaping my career and showing me the power of believing in someone.

Inspiration also comes from the desire to give back. The women who've supported and mentored me taught me the importance of paying it forward. Today, I strive to uplift others just as they uplifted me. Whether through Millionaire Latina, coaching clients, or simply lending a listening ear, my goal is to be the kind of mentor and guide my angels were for me.

One of my greatest sources of inspiration now is my business partner, Delfina. Our partnership is a story of serendipity and shared passion. We met nearly a decade ago at JP Morgan, where we worked together and formed a bond that extended far beyond the workplace. Even after our careers took us in different directions, we stayed connected, cheering each other on through life's twists and turns.

Delfina's journey is equally inspiring. Having survived thyroid cancer 14 years ago, she discovered IV therapy during her recovery and became a strong advocate for its benefits. Her passion for wellness aligned with my own, as I had seen firsthand how IV therapy helped my mom during her battle with breast cancer. Last year, when my own health challenges emerged, IV therapy became a vital part of my healing process.

It's incredible how life has a way of connecting the dots. I believe nothing is a coincidence. I call them "Diosidencias." About a year and a half ago, Delfina and I visited an IV therapy center in New York, where we met a woman running an innovative and inspiring business. We jokingly mentioned how great bringing her model to Miami would be, only to find out she was looking for partners in the area. That conversation sparked a partnership, and today, Delfina and I co-own an IV therapy center in Miami.

Delfina's unwavering belief in the power of wellness and her resilience in the face of adversity inspire me every day. Our journey together has shown me that the people you meet along the way can open doors you never imagined.

Inspiration is everywhere—in my mom's courage, the guidance of my mentors, and the partnerships that have blossomed from chance encounters. Each person, each moment, has added a layer of purpose and direction to my life. What's most exciting is knowing that the story isn't over, and more angels and opportunities are still waiting to appear.

To me, inspiration isn't just about looking up to someone; it's about being open to what they teach you and how they push you to grow. You never know who or what will lead you to your next chapter, but if you approach life with an open heart and a willingness to connect, inspiration can find you.

THE ADVICE

Throughout my life, I've collected lessons from the struggles, triumphs, and moments of quiet reflection. These experiences have shaped me into who I am today, and I want to share some of the wisdom that has carried me through. I hope that these insights resonate with you and serve as a guide when you face challenges or are uncertain about your path forward.

1. Pivot with Purpose

Life rarely goes as planned, and that's okay. One of my most important lessons is to pivot when necessary. If something isn't working, don't be afraid to change direction. Whether transitioning from medical school aspirations to a career in finance, leaving a secure corporate job to build my own business, or uprooting my life to move to Miami, each pivot brought me closer to where I was meant to be. Keep an open mind, and trust that change often leads to growth and new opportunities.

2. Never Close a Door

Every connection, every opportunity, and every experience holds value— even if you don't see it at the moment. The teacher who encouraged me to apply for a life-changing scholarship, the mentors at JP Morgan who guided my career, and the partnership with my now-business partner all stemmed from the doors I kept open. Relationships and opportunities may not pay off immediately but often lead to unexpected and extraordinary outcomes.

3. Find Mentors Everywhere

Mentorship isn't always formal, and anyone can inspire or guide you. From teachers and colleagues to friends and family, I've been blessed with people who've shared their wisdom and believed in me. Building relationships, seeking advice, and staying connected to those who support and challenge you are key. And when you have the chance, be that mentor for someone else—pay it forward by helping others find their path.

4. Grit Will Carry You

If I could tattoo one word on my wrist, it would be **grit**. Life is full of challenges, and resilience is what separates those who thrive from those who merely survive. Whether it's navigating poverty, overcoming health challenges, or starting over in a new city, grit has been my anchor. It's about not giving up, even when the odds seem insurmountable. Believe in your ability to endure and keep moving forward.

5. Embrace Evolution

We are constantly learning and evolving. The person you are today doesn't have to be the person you were yesterday. Give yourself the grace to grow, to make mistakes, and to learn from them. As I've progressed in my journey, I've discovered the power of self-reflection, gratitude, and mindfulness. These tools help me stay grounded and focused, even when life feels overwhelming.

The road hasn't been easy, but it's been worth every step. Remember, your circumstances do not define your future—your choices do. Pivot when needed, seize every opportunity, build meaningful relationships, and face life with grit and determination. Most importantly, trust that you are capable of creating a life that reflects your dreams and values.

You have everything you need within you to rise above any challenge and create a legacy of purpose and impact. The world is waiting for the brilliance only you can bring—go out there and make it happen.

THE PATH FORWARD

Follow your gut—God gave us one for a reason. It's that quiet, persistent voice that guides us even when the path feels uncertain. Trust it, because it often knows the way even before we do. Everyone has a purpose, though sometimes life's twists and turns can make it hard to see. We may need to take detours, face challenges, or even lose sight of our purpose temporarily before reconnecting with it. And that's okay. The journey itself holds the lessons that shape us, making us stronger and more prepared to fulfill our unique mission.

Be grateful for every experience—good or bad. Each one is a stepping stone that prepares you for what's ahead. My time at JP Morgan taught me invaluable leadership, strategy, and resilience lessons. Without that foundation, I wouldn't have been able to build Millionaire Latina, grow my IV Therapy business, or embark on the exciting new venture I'm starting now.

It's okay to pivot and evolve. Life isn't meant to be static, and growth often requires change. Whether it's a career shift, a new business, or a fresh outlook on life, embracing evolution keeps us aligned with our purpose and true potential.

For me, the journey of learning and challenging myself never ends. I'm committed to expanding Millionaire Latina to empower even more people to achieve financial freedom. My IV Therapy business continues to grow, addressing the crucial gap in health awareness within the Latino community. But I'm not stopping there. I'm launching a new initiative, **Biohacking Chicas**, to teach the Hispanic community how to live longer, healthier, and happier lives through non-traditional medicine and science-backed practices.

There's so much we can do to prioritize our well-being, whether it's preventative care or recovering from illness. Health isn't something we should only focus on when something goes wrong. It's a lifelong commitment to living better. Remember, just because certain health conditions run in your family doesn't mean they're inevitable. Science and technology show us that small, intentional changes can make a difference.

Today, I can confidently say I'm the healthiest I've ever been—not just in body, but in mind and spirit. It's a testament to what's possible when you follow your gut, trust your purpose, and keep pushing forward.

So here's my message to you: embrace your journey, keep learning, and don't be afraid to pivot when needed. Your purpose is waiting, and the world needs the brilliance only you can bring. Let's rise together, healthier, stronger, and ready to create joy, meaning, and impact-filled lives.

The next chapter is yours to write—make it extraordinary.

ABOUT JEANNIE

For over 23 years, Jeannie Mårmol has been driven by her passion for helping individuals and businesses achieve their financial goals. As CEO and founder of Millionaire Latina, Jeannie cultivates a broad community dedicated to fostering resilience and empowering others to attain lasting financial freedom.

As part of her mission, Jeannie demystifies finance, making it accessible, inspiring, and actionable for a diverse audience. Her multifaceted approach encompasses personalized one-on-one coaching, corporate consulting, dynamic workshops, and impactful speaking engagements.

Jeannie's career began at JPMorgan right out of college. Her most recent pivotal role as the Executive Director-Market Director at JPMorgan Chase, overseeing 11 retail locations and leading a team of 130 employees while managing $6.6 billion in assets under management, was critical during the pandemic. During her 19-year tenure, she consistently exhibited exceptional leadership skills, propelling business growth and championing opportunities for her fellow Latin community. She earned the prestigious Chase Champion award twice and the Top Manager Award four times throughout her career.

Jeannie was recognized for her outstanding contributions and was inducted into the YWCA-NYC Academy of Women Leaders in 2019 and nominated for the Top 10 Corporate Latina Executive of the Year award in 2020. In 2024, she was recognized as one of

The Latinas to Watch by ALPFA and nominated by United Latinas as Extraordinary Latina. Her commitment to empowering women within JPMorgan Chase, and now through Millionaire Latina, and Biohacking Chicas comes naturally.

Jeannie's inspirational journey began in the Dominican Republic and continued with her immigration to the US at the age of five, together with her mom. She has experienced firsthand and firmly believes in the transformative power of education, financial freedom, and mentorship as indispensable foundations for personal and professional success.

Learn more and connect with Jeannie at:
Linkedin: linkedin.com/in/jeanniemarmol
Website: jeanniemarmol.com
Instagram: jeanniemarmol and Biohacking Chicas

KALIA ZIRIANETH APARICIO PADILLA

"The world is already challenging enough; we need to be our own biggest supporters."

- Kalia Zirianeth Aparicio Padilla

~ ~ ~

Kalia, a proud Afro-Latina from Panama City, Panama, who journeyed through the vibrant neighborhoods of Santa Ana, Tocumen, and Chilibre of Panama, ultimately making her home in Texas. She embodies the spirit of change within our communities.

Known as the connector among her friends and family, Kalia radiates that same energy with her colleagues.

As a leader, she inspires through her soft yet diplomatic approach. Her fierce passion for achieving her goals propels her to uplift others on their own paths to success.

~ ~ ~

For my best friend Kevin Obed Hernandez (1992-2021), mi familia en Panamá, my pet dogs Misty and Kanela, and my loved ones and dear friends in the United States. Thank you for being my North Star.

.

FROM STRUGGLES TO STRENGTH: A JOURNEY OF GROWTH AND GRATITUDE

THE JOURNEY

My story begins in Panama, where I spent my early childhood before moving to the United States at 11. Growing up, my mother was often away, working tirelessly as a teen mom to provide for us. Her long hours made it hard for me to understand her absence. I thought she had abandoned me at the time, and this misunderstanding impacted me deeply. I became rebellious, acting out in school even though my grades were good. I was navigating emotions I couldn't fully comprehend as a child. My beloved grandmother "Mamaritza" lovingly raised me while my mom worked hard to create a better life for us in another country. Her unwavering support and nurturing spirit shaped my childhood in ways I will always cherish.

Everything began to make sense when I finally reunited with my mother in the U.S.. Seeing her sacrifices firsthand, I understood the immense challenges she faced to create a better future for us. She wasn't just working hard but also going to school, and seeing her pursue her education became a turning point in my life. It instilled in me a belief that I, too, could achieve my dreams through dedication and resilience. Her strength and commitment motivated me to pursue higher education, and I remain deeply grateful to her for teaching me to "never give up on the things that make you smile."

I also quickly learned that things were not always as they seemed from afar. After enduring domestic violence, we decided to move from Connecticut to Texas. The journey ahead was long as we had to leave most things behind and could only travel with our six boxes on a Greyhound. My mom, brother, and I built our new life in Texas in a humble but peaceful one-bedroom apartment. We shared a small TV and enjoyed our newfound joy in San Antonio. We discovered healing through the power of volunteerism and embraced adventure by actively exploring the city on weekends. One of my favorite memories of our new beginning was finally having our car—an old silver Buick with a maroon front-row bench seat that we affectionately called 'El Dinosaurio.'

While I am grateful, and despite the bumps along the way, I've had to put in the effort to rebuild my relationship with my mother. Like many in the Latino community, I've faced generational trauma and complex family dynamics that took time and effort

Taking care of your mental health is an act of self-love.

to heal. But healing was essential—not only for my personal growth but also for how I show up in the world and help others. A healthy mind is foundational to everything I've accomplished. *"Taking care of your mental health is an act of self-love."*

When I became a first-generation college student at Texas A&M, I faced one of the most significant challenges of my life. I struggled academically and personally, especially as I was undiagnosed with ADHD at the time. With newfound freedom came difficulties I wasn't prepared for, but I sought help and pushed through. College became a journey of self-discovery. It gave me the confidence to embrace who I am, to wear my big, curly hair proudly, and to speak out as my authentic self. I also found the most beautiful and meaningful friendships I will cherish forever.

I gained valuable leadership experience in college by joining organizations and becoming a proud member of Sigma Gamma Rho Sorority, Inc.. By the time I was in grad school, I was ready to tackle challenges head-on. I studied biomedical science and initially planned to attend veterinary school. However, after volunteering in a hospital, I discovered my passion for healthcare administration and pivoted my career path. Grad school allowed me to thrive academically, especially with the help of an incredible Dominican doctor who supported me through my ADHD diagnosis and treatment and a therapist who encouraged me to dig deep and love all parts of my story. This meant nurturing younger versions of myself and saying yes to the things that felt healthy in the present. By embracing the past and remaining grounded in my pursuit of success, I graduated with honors from Texas Woman's University through the Upsilon Phi Delta Honor Society, the national academic honor society for healthcare administration students in the United States.

After completing grad school, I stayed in Houston and began a career in healthcare, working across various sectors. My first job was in behavioral healthcare, serving low-income and homeless communities. That role was one of the most humbling experiences of my life, as I saw people at their most vulnerable and worked to find creative ways to help them get the resources they needed.

Later, I transitioned to public health, working in a clinic that primarily served Latino communities. There, I focused on preventative care and learned how vital early intervention is for improving health outcomes. I eventually moved into oncology, where I supported families through some of the hardest moments of their lives. This work was equally humbling, teaching me that cancer doesn't discriminate—it can touch anyone, regardless of their wealth, health, or circumstances.

Throughout my journey, I have embraced my identity as an Afro-Latina. I celebrate my culture, skin, language, hair, and roots, knowing they are essential to who I am. Like many, I have faced hardships such as sexual abuse, food insecurity, and low self-esteem, yet these challenges have strengthened my resolve to become the best version of myself. They do not define me; instead, I transform these experiences into empowerment, breaking generational patterns and inspiring other women to overcome their struggles. *"I can be changed by what happens to me. But I refuse to be reduced by it."* - Maya Angelou.

My journey has been shaped by community, family, and an unwavering belief in the power of resilience. I remind myself and others: *"Recognize your value and embrace it wholeheartedly. You deserve to be treated with the love and respect that matches your worth, so never feel compelled to settle for anything less."*

THE LEARNINGS

One of the most valuable lessons I've learned is the importance of community. Surrounding yourself with the right people—those who inspire, uplift, and support you—is critical to success. But building a strong community starts with self-love. To allow good people into your life, you must love and respect yourself enough to make space for them.

I strive to move with intention, integrity, and kindness in everything I do. These three principles have guided me personally and professionally. They've helped me build meaningful relationships and achieve success in my career. For example, I've found that genuine connections matter more than surface-level networking. When entering a room full of people, I focus on forming deeper relationships with just a few individuals rather than trying to meet everyone. This approach has been invaluable in building strong, meaningful connections that have shaped my journey.

Another key learning has been the importance of self-care. Taking care of your mental and emotional health is not a luxury—it's a necessity. Self-care means dedicating Sundays to myself, which I call "Self-Care Sundays." Whether getting a massage, a pedicure, or simply taking time to reflect, these moments prepare me for the challenges and opportunities ahead. Being intentional about self-care has made a significant difference in my ability to make better decisions and remain grounded in my personal life and at work.

Lastly, I've learned that success is not just about achieving goals but also about embracing challenges as opportunities for growth. My struggles, including being a first-generation college student, navigating an undiagnosed ADHD diagnosis, and overcoming low self-esteem, have shaped who I am today. They've taught me resilience and the importance of seeking help when needed. These experiences have fueled my confidence and made me a stronger leader.

THE INSPIRATION

I've learned the importance of having mentors who look like me and those who don't, as they can speak your name in different spaces and offer diverse perspectives.

My inspirations come from both personal relationships and public figures. In my personal life, I've been fortunate to have mentors who have been in my corner, cheering me on and guiding me through my professional journey. My mentors are Brent Lawless, Richelle Webb-Dixon, Dr. Jennifer Small, Dr. Sandy Murdock, Tyara Barge, Zach Weyand, Phillip Dorsey, Arianne Dowdell, Deborah Lee-Eddie, Jeanna

Bamburg, Colonel Kenneth Allison, Lisa Brady Barto, Dana Weston Graves, Rex Everett, Khadeja Haye, MD, and Dr. Lisa Maria Mallory, amazing leaders who have truly helped shape my career. They've supported me in my career and shown me the value of mentorship and sponsorship. I've learned the importance of having mentors who look like me and those who don't, as they can speak your name in different spaces and offer diverse perspectives.

Oprah Winfrey said, *"A mentor is someone who allows you to see the hope inside yourself."* I truly value these people in my life because they offer support, partnership, and the shared responsibility of growing together in our communities. The collaboration has truly propelled my journey and given me the confidence to succeed in all my roles. While my mentors have been invaluable, I also sincerely appreciate the support and growth I've gained from my mentees. They have been instrumental in shaping my understanding of leadership and taught me how to adapt to diverse personalities. I sincerely thank my mentees Bhumi Patel, Daniela Caisaguano, Emily Edo, and Yasmin Artis.

On a broader scale, Justice Sonia Sotomayor has been a significant source of inspiration. Despite the barriers she faced, her journey, perseverance, and achievements remind me that representation matters and that there's power in breaking through stereotypes. I often recommend her biography as a must-read for anyone seeking inspiration.

My mother stands as a beacon of inspiration in my life. Her countless sacrifices and unwavering dedication have instilled a profound sense of resilience. I have watched her navigate life's challenges with grace and strength; her example encourages me to persevere. Alongside her is my younger brother Timmy, a steadfast supporter who has always believed in me. His constant encouragement and loyalty provide a comforting presence, reminding me that I am never alone in my journey. Together, they motivate me to reach my goals and face obstacles with determination.

I also want to take a moment to acknowledge my dad, Carmelo, who entered my life when I was just 12. There's a beautiful saying that goes, *"A father is not the one who made you, but the one who raised you."* You embraced that role wholeheartedly, nurturing and loving me while blessing me with two wonderful siblings, CJ and JJ. I am genuinely grateful for the joy and love you have brought into my life. Your support has guided my journey, and I sincerely appreciate everything you have done for me.

Even my dogs have played a significant role in my life, offering companionship and comfort during tough times. Additionally, professional organizations like the National Association of Health Services Executives (N.A.H.S.E.), the National Association of Latino Healthcare Executives (NALHE), and the American College of Healthcare Executives (ACHE), have been instrumental in shaping my career and connecting me with a community of like-minded professionals.

THE ADVICE

To my younger self, I would say: slow down and show yourself grace. As a young person and a young professional, I often pushed myself too hard, trying to do too much at once. I now know that it's okay to rest and take life one step at a time. Not everything needs to be accomplished immediately, and aligning your goals with where you are in life is important. Ask yourself what's most important to you now—whether it's flexibility, financial stability, or family—and let that guide your decisions. *"Don't let the things that matter least get in the way of the things that matter most."* - Roy T. Bennett.

I would also encourage my younger self to show herself kindness. Latina women are often our own harshest critics, carrying the weight of high expectations. The world is already challenging enough; we need to be our own biggest supporters. *"When you say 'yes' to others, make sure you are not saying 'no' to yourself."* – Paulo Coelho.

I'd say, "You don't need to prove anything to anyone. You are enough." Lastly, I'd emphasize that you should know your worth and never settle for less than you deserve professionally, romantically, and personally. *"How you love yourself is how you teach others to love you."* – Rupi Kaur.

One of the most important pieces of advice I always give is to embrace who you are fully and deeply. It's okay to take up space. It's okay to pursue your dreams unapologetically. And it's okay to prioritize your happiness and well-being. Trust yourself and recognize that everything you need to succeed is already within you. *"Always stay true to yourself and never let what somebody says distract you from your goals."* – Michelle Obama.

THE PATH FORWARD

For me, the path forward is about paying it forward. In my personal life, I want to continue creating meaningful experiences for my family and friends. I aim to expose them to opportunities and spaces where they may not always see themselves represented, helping to build memories and foster a sense of possibility.

Professionally, I aspire to mentor, teach, and inspire others, much like my mentors have done for me. I want to help others grow, reach their goals, and realize their potential. Becoming a professor and continuing to connect with people in meaningful ways are part of my long-term goals. I hope to be the kind of leader who provides opportunities and guidance, encouraging others to push past challenges and achieve their dreams. *"There is no investment you can make which will pay you so well as the effort to scatter sunshine and good cheer through your establishment."* -Orison Swett Marden.

But I'm also learning to embrace stillness. Life doesn't always need to be a race; there's beauty in pausing, observing, and appreciating the present moment. Moving forward, I hope to continue building a life that blends ambition with mindfulness, always staying true to my values and uplifting those around me.

ABOUT KALIA

Kalia Z. Aparicio is a Panama City, Panama native who graduated from Texas A&M University with a Bachelor of Science in Biomedical Science and a Certificate in International Cultural Competency and Spanish, a Master's in Healthcare Administration from Texas Woman's University, a Certification in Healthcare Innovation from Arizona State University, and a Certification in Public Health from Georgia Southern University.

Kalia is committed to emotional intelligence in leadership, enhancing patient and clinician experiences, and building culturally inclusive partnerships. She is a UNITED LATINAS Ambassador and is involved with several organizations, including the American College of Healthcare Executives (ACHE), the National Association of Health Services Executives (N.A.H.S.E.), the National Association of Latino Healthcare Executives (NALHE), and the Health Information and Management Systems Society (HIMSS), receiving multiple awards for her contributions including

- Sigma Gamma Rho Sorority, Inc.:
  - National Education Fund Academic Award
  - Undergraduate Community Service Award
  - Undergraduate Lecia Swain Ross Leadership Award
- American College of Healthcare Executives:
  - Southeast Texas Chapter Outstanding Community Contribution Award
  - Southeast Texas Chapter David J. Fine Academic Award
  - Southeast Texas Chapter Congress on Leadership Award
- National Association of Health Services Executives:
  - Houston Chapter Member of the Year Award
  - Haynes Rice National Academic Award
- Georgia Southern University:
  - President's Volunteer Service Award
- Texas Woman's University:
  - Masters Student of Excellence Award
  - Outstanding Student Leader Award

- National Pan-Hellenic Council:
    - Houston Sorority Woman of the Year
- Healthcare Financial Management Association:
    - TX Gulf Coast Chapter Student Academic Award
- Texas A&M University
    - Buck Weirus Spirit Award

As a Pet Therapist with her Labradoodle, Misty, Kalia actively gives back to the community and serves on various boards, including the Advisory Board for the Healthcare Administration Program at Texas Woman's University and ForbesBLK. The mission of ForbesBLK is to champion a global community of Black entrepreneurs, professionals, leaders, and creators that are driving systematic change in business, culture, and society.

Kalia also recently founded the San Antonio Chapter of NALHE in November 2024. Kalia has ten years of experience as a business operations strategist in healthcare and is the Director of Provider Services in her current role, overseeing the onboarding, credentialing, and scheduling of +600 clinicians in General Surgery, Acute Behavioral Health, Orthopedics, Obstetrics and Gynecology, and Ambulatory specialties. Kalia is very supportive of DEI (Diversity, Equity, and Inclusion) initiatives because she believes they are an excellent way to support her teammates and learn more about the world. She actively participates in the committees and events for the Black Cultural, Women in Leadership, Veterans, LGBTQ+ Allies, and Hispanic/Latinx Resource Groups at her workplace.

As a scholar Kalia, co-authored a publication in the Journal of Oncology, which focused on the first use of telehealth for cancer patients during COVID-19. Kalia continuously seeks opportunities to learn and grow, participating in programs that not only enhance her skills but also allow her to give back to the community. These include the Houston Hispanic Chamber of Commerce's Emerging Leaders Institute (Class of 2019), Korn Ferry's Leadership University for Humanity (Cohort 14-1), NALHE's La Mesa Leadership Program (2021 Inaugural Cohort), and Texas Woman's University's Partnership with the Jane Nelson Institute for Women's Leadership and the Greater Houston Women's Chamber of Commerce's Bold LeadHERship Roundtable (Houston Cohort #2).

Kalia values inclusion and finding joy in everything she is involved in. As a foodie and a member of the Yelp Elite Squad, Kalia relishes a good brunch and enjoys trying out new spots. As an avid adventurer, Kalia loves appreciating new cultures by traveling. Kalia is also an Ambassador and Moderator for Black Women Who, which empowers, educates, and inspires women of color to hold space in outdoor environments where they're rarely seen. The organization focuses on educating women and businesses about the importance of implementing diversity, inclusiveness, and equality through recreational activities. She genuinely enjoys bringing positive energy to outdoor activities and introducing her loved ones to new experiences. These activities include: Yoga | Hiking | Camping | Pilates | Range Day | Cycling | Urban Run Club | Kayaking | Basketball | Beach Activities | Boxing | Sand Volleyball | Flag Football | Lifting | Spas, Saunas, Sound Baths | Plants.

She finds fulfillment in giving back through mentorship and elevating healthcare services that help communities navigate through health inequities. Her mission is to impact the world with kindness and tenacity. She lives by her favorite quote from Martin Luther King, Jr. "Everybody can be great because anybody can serve. You don't have to have a college degree to serve. You don't have to make your subject and verb agree to serve. You only need a heart full of grace. A soul generated by love."

Learn more and connect with Kalia at:

Website: https://linktr.ee/kalia.z.aparicio

LISSETH ZOUHBI

"Surround yourself with people that inspire, uplift you and challenge you to become the best version of yourself."

\-   Lisseth Zouhbi

~ ~ ~

Lisseth is currently the CHRO for a large non-profit in Los Angeles called Child Care Resource Center. She has almost 25 years of Human Resources experience working predominately in luxury hospitality and pivoted to non-profit nearly 3 years ago. She is passionate about developing others and supporting our community. Her background in HR includes talent management, learning & development, total rewards, DEI, organizational development, employee relations, compliance, and talent acquisition.

~ ~ ~

I dedicate this to my husband and family for always being there for me.

To my son and daughter, my dream is for you to live a life that you dream of and never give up because you are special…. I love you. "Take those risks and live your life to your fullest potential."

To all the incredible leaders and teams I have worked with, and those who have inspired me to never give up and believe in myself.

"Life is a journey and it's not just about the destination, but how we get there that shapes us into who we are as individuals."

EMBRACING THE JOURNEY: LESSONS IN LEADERSHIP, RESILIENCE, AND SELF-BELIEF

THE JOURNEY

My parents immigrated from Mexico to the U.S. in search of a better life for their children. My dad worked two to three jobs throughout my childhood to provide for our family, while my mom stayed home to care for us. It was important for our parents that we focused on our education so that we could have a better life. Hard work and dedication were vital lessons that I learned from my parents. My mom would always say to me, "Don't give up and give it all that you got."

When I graduated high school, I wanted to pursue a college degree, and I had to work several jobs to pay for college. Even though I did not have the typical U.S. college experience, nor did I finish in an average of four years, it made me appreciate my degree even more when I finally graduated with my bachelor's degree. The positive impact of juggling work and school was that I also gained work experience, which helped me fast-track my career once I graduated and deepened my appreciation for the value of continuous education.

By the time I graduated from college, my career path had shifted toward Human Resources, and I knew I wanted to reach the highest professional level in the field. This was another pivotal point in my life where someone saw my potential and mentored me in this field. My mentor's support motivated me to become the same type of transformational leader and has led me to my passion for developing others. He taught me the critical fundamentals of Human Resources, the importance of ethics in this field, and how to effectively balance the employee and business needs to succeed in this career.

As I progressed through my career, there were people who doubted my capabilities and told me directly that I would never be able to break the glass ceiling, but guess what? I did, and I am proud to say that I am the 1% of Latinas at a C-Suite level! I knew I was ready to move to the next Sr. HR level, as I was already taking on additional responsibilities, and I voiced my interest in taking the next step up in my career. However, the lack of support and trust to take on this role became evident when I was not given the opportunity. So, I decided that instead of feeling discouraged, I would not give up pursuing that next level up.

At that moment in my life, I was more determined than ever to prove to myself that I had the skills and capabilities to be an HR Executive. My career in Human Resources started as an HR Generalist and moved my way up to Manager, Director, Sr Corporate Director, Global VP of HR, and now Chief Human Resources. The different roles allowed me to work in all areas of Human Resources and not only experience in California but at a national and global level.

Now that I have reached a C-Suite level position, the focus is more on strategy, driving influence, currently leading a team of about 50, navigating business decisions that have an impact across the organization with a focus on the impact on the employees and a strategic business partner to the CEO and Senior Executives.

Becoming a mom was life-changing, as my kids inspired me to pass on the values my parents had taught me while also revealing new strengths I never knew I had. Juggling being a wife, mom, and boss is not easy. I'm blessed to have a husband and family who support me in many ways so that I am still able to achieve my personal and professional goals.

THE LEARNINGS

One of the most pivotal challenges I faced was imposter syndrome and overcoming self-doubt that I could do the job. Throughout my career, people were skeptical that I could do the job because I was a female, a minority, and a young executive.

I recall sitting in executive meetings surrounded by people who were different from me, wondering if I was skilled enough to be in that room and position.

I honestly didn't know what imposter syndrome was until recently, when it became a more commonly discussed topic, and I realized how many of us have experienced it. But back then, I didn't know how to talk about it or how to manage it. I internalized much self-doubt, but I decided to focus on what I could learn and develop new skills to demonstrate that I was qualified to do the job and take on the challenge.

I remember sitting in an executive meeting for the first time, observing the interactions among fellow executives and thinking, "Wow, this is where the key business decisions that impact the people are made!" How can I position myself to be respected as a subject matter expert and support the organization in fulfilling its goals?"

From these initial vital questions, I began to pay close attention to what was going on around me. I learned three key lessons:

1. Build a rapport with all the stakeholders at all levels, regardless of their position.
2. Gather my facts and take a position on issues.
3. Stay true to my values and who I am.

In every leadership role I've held, I've learned from my mistakes and built upon the lessons gained from the role itself, my leaders, my team, and the organization. These experiences have shaped me into the leader I am today, and I know I am still growing.

Having a close support network has been instrumental in bouncing ideas, sharing best practices, and motivating me to stay focused. I remember someone telling me that the higher you go up in the corporate ladder, the lonelier it gets, and it's true. Your responsibilities are higher, and the level of confidential/sensitive information you have to manage elevates the level of integrity that you need to have.

Despite the challenges and moments of self-doubt, I've come to realize that growth is a continuous journey. Each experience—both the victories and the setbacks—has contributed to my development as a resilient and values-driven leader. I've learned that true leadership is not about perfection but about perseverance, authenticity, and the willingness to keep evolving. As I continue to grow, I remain committed to inspiring others to face their own challenges with courage and to believe in the power of their potential.

THE INSPIRATION

There are several important people in my life who have been my inspiration.

First, my husband has played a significant role in my personal and professional success. He has always been there to support me and offer advice that has guided me in making critical decisions. He is a humble man who constantly strives to support his team and family. For him, it's not about the title you hold but how you inspire others.

Second, my parents have also been pivotal in my life. Their unwavering support has helped me balance my personal and professional responsibilities. Hard work and dedication are lessons I learned from them and have carried into every aspect of my life.

Third, my mentor took a leap of faith in me, introducing me to the field of Human Resources. He believed in me and inspired me to be resourceful, factual, and always care for our employees. He taught me that if you can inspire even one person to be their best, then you are on the right path.

I have been fortunate to have had amazing bosses throughout my career, each teaching me valuable leadership lessons. Being an effective boss doesn't mean micromanaging your team; instead, it means empowering them to make decisions and carry your vision forward. I learned that building a team with a diverse set of skills is a tremendous asset and that surrounding yourself with individuals who support you is crucial.

There are many great resources I have used throughout my career, including certifications, workshops, seminars, books, and online tools. Continuous learning and a curiosity to never stop growing have been essential to my success.

In the end, it's the connections we make and the impact we have on one another that truly define our legacy.

Reflecting on the people and experiences that have shaped my journey, I am deeply grateful for the wisdom, support, and inspiration that have guided me along the way. Each lesson and every bit of encouragement has not only contributed to my growth but has also fueled my desire to lift others as I continue to grow. In the end, it's the connections we make and the impact we have on one another that truly define our legacy.

THE ADVICE

Some advice I would give my younger self is to not be too hard on myself and give yourself grace to take a break to come back stronger. I always felt that I had to exceed expectations because I had to prove to others that I could do it. Once I achieved a goal, I was thinking of what was next without really enjoying what I had just achieved. I learned that the only person I need to compete with is myself and to celebrate the wins and learn from my failures. Take a break and enjoy the moments because life moves on very quickly.

If you don't take the risk, you'll never know what the outcome could be...so go for it! There were times when the result of taking those risks wasn't what I had hoped for, but every risk taught me something valuable. You'll never know the outcome unless you give it a shot. What's the worst that can happen? I'd rather say to myself, "I tried it and learned from it," than live with the regret of never having tried at all.

Empower yourself with knowledge. This was also critical in my career to ensure that I gained skills to advance in my career and become a more effective leader. Never underestimate the power of knowledge because no one will take that away from you.

We are in a constant world of change nowadays, and if you can adapt quickly and embrace change, you will succeed. This became more important when my children were born. I had to learn that things will not go as planned and that the most essential thing in life was to enjoy the moments with your loved ones. Life is not always "picture perfect" as we may envision it, and that's okay. We need to be able to pivot and adapt to the changes that life may present.

I have also learned that I need to take care of myself in order to give my best to others. It's okay to take a break from life's daily demands and focus on yourself. My health seems to have always been on the back burner, and this year I finally learned that we only get one life, one body, and we better take care of ourselves.

THE PATH FORWARD

We are the writers of our destiny, and every day we make choices that impact our lives. It's up to us to determine the path we want to take. Taking risks has always been a part of the choices I made, and I've learned so much from those opportunities.

We are the writers of our destiny, and every day we make choices that impact our lives.

I hope to inspire other Latinas working to break the glass ceiling to never give up. Take those risks, and don't let self-doubt overshadow your dreams and aspirations. Learn from both your failures and successes, because that's how we continue to grow and evolve. We get to write our own story every day, so embrace the challenges, savor the special moments, and celebrate your successes. Always, always keep your dreams alive.

ABOUT LISSETH

Lisseth is currently the CHRO for a large non-profit in Los Angeles called Child Care Resource Center. She has demonstrated a proven track record of success in developing and implementing HR strategies that align with the company's objectives and goals. Lisseth has almost 25 years Human Resources experience working predominately in luxury hospitality and pivoted to non-profit nearly 3 years ago. She is passionate about developing others and supporting our community. Her background in HR includes talent management, learning & development, total rewards, DEI, organizational development, employee relations, compliance and talent acquisition. She is bilingual in Spanish and has experience working with local, national and global organizations.

Lisseth graduated from California State University with a bachelor's in international business management, SHRM-CP certified, and has obtained several HR Executive certifications through eCornell and most recently the CHRO Program through the Wharton Executive Education. She is a DEI Council Member for NHRA-LA, member of Latina in the Boardroom - National Steering Committee and Executive Advisor for the Latinas Rising Up in HR Ambassador Program.

She was featured in Hispanic Executive, awarded the Top 50 Women CHRO of 2024 by Women We Admire, nominated as a finalist for the 2024 and 2025 Top 100 HR Professional Award, won the 2024 Top 50 Human Resources Team and most recently a co-author for Vol III of Latinas Rising Up in HR.

Learn more and connect with Lisseth at:

Linkedin: https://www.linkedin.com/in/lisseth-zouhbi-33406a9/
Email: Lisseth@zouhbi.com

MERCEDES SULLIVAN

"No Day But Today."

- Mercedes Sullivan

~ ~ ~

Mercedes D. Sullivan is an executive with a passion for driving growth, transformation, innovation, and inclusion. She blends over 20 years of expertise across technology, human resources, portfolio management, and social impact to resolve critical problems facing organizations today.

~ ~ ~

To my husband, Ryan, and my sons, Liam and Julian—your love and support keep me grounded and make everything possible. Finally, special thanks to the one who's given me the most: mi mamá, Mercedes. Your strength, love, and guidance planted the roots of everything I've bloomed into today.

STRENGTH THROUGH VULNERABILITY: REDEFINING SUCCESS AND TAKING UP SPACE

THE JOURNEY

I was born in Mexico City but grew up in Acapulco. I am very proud of my roots and feel it was an enormous privilege to grow up surrounded by our incredible human warmth, food, and culture. But as a determined young girl who became serious about tennis as an 8-year-old, navigating the social structure that specified girls and women should be subservient, quiet ("calladita te ves mas bonita"), and temper their ambitions, my drive felt at odds with what was deemed acceptable.

At just ten years old, I won my first national tennis championship. As I enjoyed more success on the court in the following years, the undertow of unsolicited feedback from (mostly) well-meaning friends, family, and even strangers dragged on me. My muscles were 'too masculine'; my dreams were 'too ambitious,' and talking about my wins earned me the label of being 'too outspoken' (no presumas!).

When I dropped out of high school to travel the world for competitions, the whispers grew louder. I was 'throwing away my future.' Questions followed: *Are you not going to get an education? What will people think about a young girl traveling the world alone?* Later, when I received a scholarship to an elite American college, my Mexican community felt relieved that I 'came to my senses' to return to school. It would be easier to find a husband there, they said.

Arriving in the U.S. with my new identity as a Latina immigrant, I found myself navigating yet another set of expectations. Too warm. Too friendly. Too much. It was always as though no matter what I did, I was 'doing it wrong.' I finally understood the 'ni de aqui ni de alla' – that peculiar sense that we neither entirely belong in our country of birth nor our country of residence. Initially, I struggled to bridge the gap between there and here, but as I've grown older, my perspective changed: the 'in-between' is uniquely a place of belonging. Is it easy? Not always. But it's what I have, and what I CAN control is to make the best of it.

Now, as a Latina in the corporate world, I know how important it is to see others like us in leadership and influence – because I look around, and I don't yet see enough of us. Growing up, I had few role models who looked like me, talked like me, or came from similar backgrounds. This fuels my desire to become a visible example of what's possible. I want Latinas—whether they're just starting their careers or making a pivot like I did—to see themselves in stories like mine and realize that the barriers we face can be overcome and that we have the right to take up as much space as we want.

My journey has been a series of twists and turns, each shaping the person I am today. A significant economic crisis early in my life forced me to reckon with politics and economics and reassess my goals and aspirations. At Boston College, I pursued Theology and Philosophy with plans to become a nun and reform the Catholic Church—an academic advisor deemed my ambitions "too radical for the church." It was a pivotal moment that made me question my path.

After careful consideration, I switched focus and chose to study International Political Economy, a subject that fed my growing interest in humanism and global systems. I didn't abandon Theology and Philosophy entirely, keeping those subjects as electives and continuing to study them on the side to this day. My thesis on Latin American pension systems and adulthood poverty reinforced my experience of the profound impact of economic policies on people's lives, especially the most vulnerable. This period of intense academic growth also saw me transitioning from speaking broken English to fluency—a personal triumph that underscored the power of perseverance.

Post-college, my path took several more surprising turns. I put down my competitive tennis racket to coach tennis at a Harvard summer camp, ran two marathons, and got married. After a few years of working, I continued my education in Australia. I built an off-grid, sustainable prototype house—a project I still dream of revisiting. In my professional career, I started as a Research Associate at the Corporate Executive Board (CEB, now Gartner) and quickly rose to Head of Financial Services Research, where I managed over 2,000 projects annually. I also dabbled further in entrepreneurship, building an e-commerce boutique retail business with friends, and got into consulting.

Then, my father passed away unexpectedly, and life shifted dramatically. This led to an extended career break: to mourn, to be with my mother, and to spend time with my two new babies.

When I returned to the workforce, I prioritized working for a mission-driven company and finding opportunities in Human Resources. After dozens of rejections for HR roles, I pivoted. I restarted my career as a Senior IT Business Analyst at TIAA despite having no IT experience. In IT, I learned so much, so quickly that there was no other choice. Soon after that, I moved into an IT Program Manager role. At the same time, volunteering at a hospice also gave me a deeper insight into human resilience and compassion.

Eventually, I transitioned to HR, making a lateral move to the HR PMO and working on digital portfolio delivery. I've since risen to Vice President, leading agile HR productization and delivery. Today, I am VP, HR Storefront Architect, redesigning and governing the AI-enabled employee experience, blending my passion for people with technological innovation.

Each chapter of my journey—whether on the tennis court, in the classroom, or in the corporate boardroom—has taught me to embrace my authenticity, lean into resilience, and rewrite the narratives imposed on me. My story is a testament to the power of persistence and the belief that we are not defined by where we start but by how we choose to navigate the twists and turns along the way.

We belong everywhere, and our voices, dreams, and ambitions are not *too much*. They are exactly what the world needs.

THE LEARNINGS

Growing up as an athlete traveling the world, I quickly learned how to adapt to new environments and problem-solve on the fly. I often traveled alone as a teenager and in places where not everyone spoke Spanish, so I had to figure things out independently. Those early experiences taught me resilience, to ask for help when needed, and the confidence to navigate uncertainty.

A few years later, one of my biggest challenges came when I moved to the U.S. for college. My English was still quite basic then, so I relied heavily on a dictionary and a few tutors to catch up (no Google or AI then!). It was a challenging period. Far from home, family, friends, and my culture, I experienced depression for the first time in my life. Seeking counseling was a pivotal moment for me, as it allowed me to begin unpacking deeper personal issues I hadn't yet addressed. Having an objective voice to guide me through this significant life change was both challenging and liberating, and it is a practice I still maintain.

Entering the corporate world as a Latina presented a whole new set of challenges. There was little to no representation of Latinas in leadership positions in my organization (or around me), leaving me without role models to guide my career. I often felt the unspoken pressure to hide parts of my authentic self to fit into corporate norms. Looking back, that internal conflict weighed heavily on me.

Being true to myself meant I could pivot from rejection in environments where I didn't fit, leading me to spaces where I could thrive without self-abandonment and grow authentically.

It took time to overcome these struggles, but leaning on the foundational resilience I developed from my tennis career was vital. I embraced radical honesty and authenticity, which was a game-changer. Being true to myself meant I could pivot from rejection in environments where I didn't fit, leading me to spaces where I could thrive without self-abandonment and grow authentically.

THE INSPIRATION

My parents were my foundation early on—their unwavering strength and support made me believe I could achieve anything. My maternal grandfather, a Spanish Civil War refugee who sought asylum in Mexico, was also a guiding figure. He taught me to stay true to my values, emphasizing the importance of purpose and leaving the world better than we found it by fighting for social justice.

As I grew older, I began finding inspiration in the people around me—fellow tennis players and coaches who worked tirelessly alongside me to reach our goals and special colleagues who cheered each other in pursuit of common objectives. These relationships reinforced my belief in hard work, resilience, and the power of community.

Today, I draw the most inspiration from the collective strength of women, particularly Latinas, who push through barriers and carve out spaces in worlds that often try to limit them. Watching women rise, transform, and lead motivates me to do the same in my own journey.

Spending quality time with my husband and children, nature, travel, and the flavors of the world also provide grounding for me—when times are challenging, I turn to these moments of joy and connection with the world around me for strength.

THE ADVICE

Looking back, the most valuable advice I could offer my younger self is: "Breathe. You are enough." In a world constantly pushing for the next significant achievement, I wish I had understood earlier the importance of slowing down, pausing to reflect, and giving myself grace.

In a world constantly pushing for the next significant achievement, I wish I had understood earlier the importance of slowing down, pausing to reflect, and giving myself grace.

It took time for me to realize that patience isn't about waiting—it's about trusting that new challenges give rise to new opportunities as everything unfolds.

As I've grown, I've learned that staying true to myself, my values and my goals is non-negotiable. Never expect external validation or outcomes to fill you—those are inside jobs. This inner alignment is what drives everything else.

Somewhere along the way, I was asked the simple question: "How do you want your days to feel?" That question forced me to rethink how I approach life. Instead of chasing achievements, I began to focus on living each day with presence, inner peace, and authentic connection.

I prioritize my holistic health, nurturing my mental, physical, spiritual, and emotional well-being. Radical acceptance of myself and others has allowed me to form more profound, meaningful connections without needing to "fix" things.

Maximizing life experiences has become my north star—collecting moments of joy through flavors, travels, and immersive time in nature while continuing to nerd out on learning. I've learned to prioritize experiences over material things and to be intentional about how and with whom I spend my time and energy.

Finally, to anyone embarking on a similar journey, I'd remind you: never abandon yourself. The path may be winding but staying true to yourself and taking small, consistent steps toward your goals will always lead you in the right direction.

And, don't forget to wear sunscreen!

THE PATH FORWARD

Latinas deserve to take up space. We deserve to dream big. Every glass ceiling above us is going to shatter—and soon. Our journeys are valid, our ambitions are worthy, and in any room we walk into, we belong. By sharing my story, I hope to encourage others to lean into the discomfort of being the first or only one in the room and to trust that our voices, passions, and dreams are powerful enough to reshape any space we enter.

I want Latinas—whether they're just starting their careers or making a bold pivot like I did—to see themselves in stories like mine and realize that the barriers we face can be overcome. We have the right to take up as much space as we want. There is no reason to minimize our expectations. We can be top athletes, tech executives, business owners, or anything else we aim to achieve. It's time we own that and stop shrinking ourselves to fit into the assumptions of others.

We contain multitudes, and we are ready to be seen and heard. The world where more Latinas feel empowered to lead, innovate, and pursue their boldest dreams unapologetically is the world I want to live in. It is both a privilege and a responsibility to have a hand in shaping that world.

I want my legacy to be one of strength through vulnerability. By sharing my story, I hope other Latinas will see that they can succeed, no matter how non-traditional their path may be.

My call to action is simple: Find your inner strength, but don't spurn the collective power of community. Ask for help when needed, be open to new perspectives, and always lead with love.

Together, we can dream, achieve, and leave a lasting impact—because we belong and we are ready.

ABOUT MERCEDES

Mercedes D. Sullivan is the VP, People Transformation at McKinley Companies. Prior to this role, she served as VP, Storefront Architect, for the People Team at TIAA, a leading provider of secure retirement income solutions. In this capacity, she led the development and continuous improvement of AI-enabled employee experiences.

At TIAA Mercedes also held the position of VP, Head of People Team PMO, where she led HR productization, agile transformation, and project delivery.

Before TIAA, she held program delivery leadership roles at Symphonic Strategies, a social impact consultancy, and was Head of Financial Services Custom Research at CEB (now Gartner), providing best practice research and advice to over 600 global financial institutions.

Born in Mexico City and raised in Acapulco, Mexico, Mercedes was a national tennis champion, achieving a top 30 world junior tennis ranking. She later attended Boston College on a tennis scholarship.

Mercedes holds undergraduate and graduate degrees in International Studies from Boston College and the University of Sydney, Australia, respectively.

Through her professional and personal experience, Mercedes embodies her commitment to enabling individuals and teams to thrive, win, and feel included in the marketplace.

Learn more and connect with Mercedes at:
      Linkedin: https://www.linkedin.com/in/mercedessullivan/

MILDRED ESPINOZA

"The Sky is the Limit!"

\- Mildred Espinoza

~ ~ ~

Mildred Espinoza is a two-time Emmy Award-winning journalist, television executive producer, and entrepreneur with over 25 years of experience in media, communication, and international affairs. Originally from Guatemala, she built a distinguished career in New York City, producing content for renowned outlets such as MSNBC, NBC/Telemundo, CNN en Español, Mega TV and Bloomberg Television. Her Emmy-winning documentary, Guatemala, La Joya de Centro América, exemplifies her dedication to showcasing her homeland's beauty and culture. Recognized globally for her expertise in media and communication, Mildred has shared her knowledge at high-level conferences across the Americas, Asia, and Europe. As the founder of Empowering Business Latin America (EBLA), she provides strategic media training, digital marketing, and communication services to clients in Guatemala and the U.S. A professor, motivational speaker, and philanthropist, she remains committed to education and social impact. Currently, she divides her time between Guatemala and the United States, working on her second book to inspire others to achieve their goals with her guiding motto: "The sky is the limit.

~ ~ ~

I wholeheartedly dedicate this chapter to God, my beloved husband, my strong and amazing mother, my siblings, family, cherished friends, supportive colleagues, and wise mentors—each of whom has played a pivotal role in shaping my journey. Everything I have achieved over the years has stemmed from the encouragement of those who have believed in me. I am deeply grateful to everyone who has entered my life, enabling me to dream and pursue those dreams boldly, even in the face of challenges and uncertainties. Additionally, I would like to express my appreciation to United Latinas for the privilege of contributing to this extraordinary book, which empowers women to shine and inspire others. I am thankful to all who have crossed my path.

EMBRACING THE JOURNEY: A "FEAR LESS" STRATEGY FOR TAKING CHARGE OF YOUR OBJECTIVES

THE JOURNEY

The Journey of an Aspiring Youth

Arriving in New York City as a seven-year-old Guatemalan immigrant in 1981 was an overwhelming experience filled with conflicting feelings. Initially, I was excited about being in the Big Apple. Still, I faced the challenge of not speaking English, leaving me uncertain about navigating my new school and what lay ahead. However, I was fortunate to encounter incredible teachers like Mrs. Damiani, Mrs. Rivera, and Mrs. González at Public School 46 in Fort Greene, Brooklyn. They saw not my limitations but my potential, often calling me "a young girl with fire in her belly." They instilled the thrill of success, encouraging me to embrace my Hispanic heritage through competitions and music. Their unwavering support became the bedrock for my journey.

Another pivotal moment came from Mrs. Cohen at Queen of All Saints Catholic School, who devoted her lunch hours to helping me improve my reading skills. Her dedication ignited my love for literature and ultimately guided me toward a career in broadcast journalism. Alongside a hardworking mother who always reminded me that "the sky is the limit," these experiences shaped my "Fear Less" attitude.

The Power of a "Fear Less" Approach

Those enlightening moments of realization inspired me to chase what once felt like "el sueño imposible"—a dream that, through unwavering dedication, fervor, and a brave spirit, transformed into tangible achievements. My story is not unique; it mirrors the journeys of countless successful Latinas across the United States, whose narratives have been and will continue to be celebrated in this extraordinary book.

I share my childhood experiences not to highlight my differences but to illuminate the timeless values instilled in me at home—values that transcend time and remain profoundly significant in our lives. The lessons learned in my youth—embracing responsibility, putting in hard work, showing respect for others, demonstrating loyalty, remaining consistent, and embodying honesty—ignited a Fear Less determination in adulthood. I recognized that these core values were the non-negotiable elements essential for building trust and credibility on my path to success.

Conquer Mountains

My aspiration to become a journalist in New York City was deeply rooted in a desire to serve the public. I embarked on my television broadcasting journey in the general market. Still, when the chance arose to give back to my community, I consciously pivoted to the Hispanic market with NBC/Telemundo 47. The weighty responsibility of a journalist is to educate and inform the public, yet I felt an even deeper obligation to uplift Latino families understanding the dreams and aspirations of immigrants in the United States.

As an Executive Producer, I experienced immense joy in informing the Hispanic community in the tri-state area of New York and equipping them with essential tools to thrive in a land far from their roots. Whether it was guiding them in starting small businesses, navigating immigration laws, managing finances, or securing educational opportunities for their children, I was acutely aware of the hopes hardworking parents held for their children in America. This realization fueled my desire to do more. As I evolved in my career, embracing a Fear Less approach to reinvention, I discovered the beauty of "glocal" initiatives, bridging the needs of a Guatemalan audience with their loved ones in New York.

This endeavor marked the inception of Empowering Business Latin America (EBLA), my own video production, media, communication, and coaching enterprise in Guatemala. Today, this company creates local jobs, contributing to job creation in the country and hopefully helping to mitigate migration to the United States. Furthermore, we have forged partnerships with U.S. private and non-profit organizations dedicated to advancing educational and sports initiatives, virtual health, as well as improving communication and image in the nursing sector across both the United States and Latin America.

Our mission is ongoing, as we strive to build a legacy that extends beyond personal achievement, sharing knowledge, and creating opportunities for current and future generations in both regions.

THE LEARNINGS

Adapt and Harness Optimism

Today, I wholeheartedly attribute my journey to the powerful "fear less" mindset that has served as the cornerstone for embracing a diverse culture. This approach has empowered me to navigate my career with strategy and creativity. By adopting this perspective, I have fostered my professional development and unlocked a world of possibilities, reaching beyond the borders of the United States to include vibrant regions like Latin America.

> *We possess an incredible ability to adapt and thrive when we harness a spirit of optimism.*

Throughout my professional journey, I have been fortunate enough to explore nearly 20 countries. One crucial lesson learned in unfamiliar environments is that we possess an incredible ability to adapt and thrive when we harness a spirit of optimism, fueling our decisions with a resolute "yes, I can" attitude. Research from UCLA highlights that our past experiences significantly shape our optimistic outlooks. Indeed, optimism emerges from our social interactions, spreading like a contagion among those we connect with.

Training our minds to cultivate an optimistic view of life and our aspirations can pave the way for positive results. This approach is invaluable, especially when we face obstacles. Let's embrace this empowering perspective and transform challenges into stepping stones toward our dreams.

Thrive Amidst Adversity

In 2006, I embarked on a transformative journey, stepping away from the comfort of my successful television career to embrace the path of entrepreneurship. At the pinnacle of my professional life, I felt a powerful urge to dive into the world of business in the vibrant landscape of New York

City, confident in the credibility I had built within the television industry. This bold move led me to produce pilots for various television stations, catering to both General and Hispanic markets.

As I navigated the entrepreneurial waters, I found myself providing documentary content for my former employer, NBC Telemundo, while also stepping into roles as a publicist and career coach for colleagues and clients alike. Despite the ominous signs of an impending recession, which culminated in the Great Recession of 2008—resulting in over 8 million job losses in the United States, as the Department of Labor reported—I chose a different path. While many might have seen this crisis as a reason to retreat into the safety of employment, I instead adopted a "Fear Less" mindset, allowing me to thrive amidst adversity.

What could have been a setback transformed into a remarkable opportunity for both my personal and professional growth as an entrepreneur. My former colleagues began seeking my guidance on how to reinvent themselves, which inspired me to develop a coaching product and pursue content creation opportunities beyond New York and the U.S., ultimately leading me back to my roots in Guatemala, where I needed to adapt to a new culture, familiarize myself with different idioms, navigate my surroundings, and embrace a distinct lifestyle at a slower pace than what I was used to in New York City, a place known for its relentless energy and constant activity. However, as the saying goes, if you can make it in New York, you can make it anywhere.

This experience exemplifies the ongoing changes we face in the business world. As entrepreneurs, it's essential to maintain an open mindset and adaptability. To achieve success, I needed to understand the business culture in Guatemala. Fortunately, my prior business experience was beneficial; however, I needed to rebuild from the ground up. Despite these challenges, I remained committed to my objective of giving back to Guatemala by sharing the professional skills and knowledge I had acquired in the U.S. in addition to building new relationships.

Thinking outside the box may sound cliché, but stepping beyond our comfort zones often reveals our hidden potential as innovative problem solvers and doers. This creative pursuit of opportunities culminated in finding my first business investor, new clients, and my second Emmy Award for the documentary "Guatemala La Joya de Centro América" (Guatemala: The Jewel of Central America), a testament to the power of resilience and exploration.

THE INSPIRATION

Now, let me share a profound truth: my journey was never taken without the guiding light of a compass. That compass has always been mentorship. I cherish the memories of my teachers and the invaluable lessons they imparted. From the earliest days of my education, I recognized the vital role that mentors play, a realization that has accompanied me throughout my professional path.

Mentors are the unsung heroes who work tirelessly behind the scenes in our lives. Over the years, I have actively sought mentors across various domains: personal growth, spiritual awakening, career advancement, and business acumen. How have I embraced Fear Lessness in my mentorship journey? By choosing to reach out without hesitation. However, I didn't just approach anyone; I sought those who embodied specific qualities. These qualities include shared values, a proven history of success, unwavering commitment, discipline, and, above all, a sincere and unconditional desire to uplift others.

It is crucial to have a diverse array of mentors. We all require external guidance, which helps illuminate our paths. So, when you find yourself in need of direction, take the time to research and connect with the finest mentors—individuals with varied backgrounds and expertise who can significantly enhance your journey toward success.

THE ADVICE

In addition to seeking external guidance for my personal development, I discovered the importance of embracing habits and practices that fuel my enthusiasm for overcoming the next challenge. Each of us requires a consistent influx of energy and positivity to navigate our daily lives, especially when faced with inevitable setbacks. It's essential to carve out time for ourselves, allowing our minds and bodies to rejuvenate, equipping us to tackle tough times, challenging meetings, and critical decisions. To truly embrace a harmonious life, it is essential for each of us to carve out moments dedicated to our rejuvenation.

Three fundamental pillars of my Fear Less, non-negotiable lifestyle keep me grounded: First, my spiritual values are paramount; they forge a profound connection with God, bringing me an indescribable sense of inner peace and clarity amidst the busyness of life and work. Second, the moments I share with my husband, our golden retriever, family, and friends are invaluable. These are the times filled with laughter and joy, sparking the release of uplifting chemicals in my brain that enhance my well-being. Lastly, I prioritize exercise, committing to working out three to four times a week, which is a powerful stress management tool.

This Fear Less approach to daily living has transformed into my refuge, nurturing creativity, resilience, and the relentless pursuit of my aspirations. It embodies the legacy I

True happiness thrives in a balanced life, achievable only when we cultivate self-love and prioritize our well-being, enabling us to offer our best selves to those around us.

wish to create—a treasured gift for humanity. Ultimately, true happiness thrives in a balanced life, achievable only when we cultivate self-love and prioritize our well-being, enabling us to offer our best selves to those around us.

THE PATH FORWARD

One of my most cherished reflections on legacy expresses, "Many tombstones could well read, 'Died at 30. Buried at 60,'" as noted by Nicholas Murray Butler.

Have you paused to reflect on where you currently stand in life—both personally and professionally? Are you at the crossroads of your dreams, or have you found yourself wandering through the maze of uncertainty? Taking a moment to consider these questions can be a powerful exercise. If you feel fulfilled and at peace, bask in that comfort. I'd love for this chapter to ignite your imagination and lead you toward even greater possibilities. However, suppose you feel stagnant or unsure of your next steps. In that case, I invite you to explore the resources that can guide you toward a thrilling new horizon, equipped with a "Fear Less" mindset that prioritizes courage over fear and empowers you to achieve more, regardless of age, time, and expectations.

By sharing my journey within these pages, I hope to inspire others to embrace a "Fear Less" philosophy. My career as a journalist, media coach, university professor, and entrepreneur has shown me that now is the time to empower those around us with practical wisdom. In a world evolving at lightning speed, we must shift from being passive observers to proactive creators. Research highlights that our innate desire for positive change can propel us to new heights—whether that means landing a promotion, launching a business, or nurturing meaningful relationships.

The key lies in embracing what I call the "Fear Less" factor—a powerful mindset that champions resilience and allows us to chase our own "sueño imposible," our "impossible dream." Let this mindset transform your outlook, and remember that the courage to dream Fear Lessly can open doors to a future filled with purpose, joy, and limitless possibilities.

So, the next time someone asks you what you do, share that you are in the business of conquering mountains with a Fear Less attitude. Remember, with courage and determination, the sky truly is the limit. Embrace your journey, pursue your dreams, and inspire others to do the same. In the end, it is worth knowing whether or not we made a difference to someone else. Together, let us strive to make the impossible possible for us and our future generations.

ABOUT MILDRED

Mildred Espinoza is a two-time recipient of the esteemed Emmy award, presented by the National Academy of Television Arts and Sciences in New York. Originally from Guatemala, she spent her formative years in New York City, where she pursued her education and built most of her professional career in the media sector as a journalist, television executive producer, and entrepreneur. Furthermore, she received a silver medal from the United Nations Correspondents Association for her contributions to sustainable tourism. In 2012, the Institute of Tourism of Guatemala (INGUAT) recognized her as a communication ambassador abroad, honoring her commitment to promoting the image of Guatemala within the United States.

Mildred Espinoza's professional prestige has been recognized on platforms such as CNN en Español, MSNBC, and NBC/Telemundo, business magazines, as well as by global entities like the Business and Professional Women (BPW), which is present in over 80 countries. This federation invited her to an international congress in Finland to share her knowledge and expertise on media, image, and communication to help strengthen women-owned business leadership at a global level. Additionally, she has been selected to participate in high-level public and private sector conferences in Guatemala, El Salvador, Honduras, Panama, Taiwan, Egypt, Brazil, and Japan where she has exchanged experiences on media, image, communication, and tourism, contributing to economic growth.

Mildred Espinoza began her media career in 1997 in New York City, starting in the general market with WPIX, Channel 11, a primary station for the CW Television Network. Her journey continued at Crain Communications, where she contributed to Pensions & Investments and Investment News, and she also held a producer role at MSNBC and for Ron Insana at CNBC. In 2003, she shifted her focus to the Hispanic market, taking on the role of Executive Producer at NBC/Telemundo 47. In this capacity, she oversaw Special Projects, which included health, business, and education franchises, international documentaries, as well as coverage of major U.S. events like political conventions, elections, and commemorations of September 11, and the United Nations General Assembly. Mildred produced the Emmy-winning documentary "Guatemala, La Joya de Centro América" ("Guatemala, The Jewel of Central America"). As a content creator and entrepreneur, her work extended to creating content for various outlets, including Bloomberg Television, Mega TV, CNN en Español, and radio station 93.1 FM in New York City.

After spending 35 years overseas, Espinoza made her way back to Guatemala, where she established Empowering Business Latin America (EBLA). Through EBLA Digital, she offers services that include media training, image and communication coaching for businesses, audiovisual production, digital marketing, and design. Her 25 years of experience in media, communication, public relations, and international affairs enable her to support both corporate and academic sectors in Guatemala and the United States.

Espinoza participates in boards and is also a Professor of Journalism and Communication at the University ISTMO, she is also an International Motivational Speaker and contributes to Hippo Hive, Institute for Virtual Health Education, a U.S.-led company.

Among her passions is philanthropy, dedicating her time to organizations focused on education. She has received humanitarian recognition from the MIR Foundation in the Dominican Republic and has supported the REMAR Foundation in Guatemala.

Espinoza completed her bachelor's degree in communication sciences at New York University, an institution that, along with the National Association of Hispanic Journalists in the United States, awarded her a scholarship. Currently, she lives between Guatemala and the United States with her husband. She is now writing her second book, to empower and inspire others to reach their personal and professional goals. Her motto is "The sky is the limit."

Learn more and connect with Mildred at:
Linkedin: linkedin.com/in/mildredespinoza
Website: https://ebladigital.com/en/
Instagram: instagram.com/mildredespi

MONICA DUPERON RODRIGUEZ

"Words are our most powerful weapon. They can cut through our spirit with negativity, or they can manifest your wildest dreams into reality."

- Monica Duperon Rodriguez

~ ~ ~

Monica Duperon Rodriguez is a distinguished security expert with over 30 years of experience in corporate security, protective services, and law enforcement. She has extensive expertise in developing and implementing security plans, protecting high-value assets, and providing executive protection globally. Monica's diverse background includes roles in human trafficking and gang task forces, undercover narcotics, and SWAT hostage negotiation. She is a respected mentor, published author, and active leader in professional security communities. Monica's work emphasizes compassion, resilience, and global initiatives in self-defense and anti-trafficking.

~ ~ ~

To my beloved family and friends, Thank you for your unwavering support, love, and encouragement throughout my journey. Your belief in me has been a constant source of strength and inspiration. This achievement is ours. A special thank you to and especially to my mother, Maria Teresa Esparza, my sister, Corina Cruz Lopez, and my forever partner, Gadi Anshel. In loving memory of my pops, Luis Angel Duperon, my Apa Pedro Cruz, and my younger brother, Randy Esparza, who passed too soon. With all my love and gratitude, forever yours, MDR

STRENGTH, HERITAGE AND HOPE: A JOURNEY BEYOND THE STRUGGLES

THE JOURNEY

My life began in an environment filled with instability. As a child, I never had the luxury of a stable home or the comfort of knowing what the next day would bring or where my next meal would come from. The chaos of my early years could have easily led me down a path of despair and resignation, making me a permanent victim of my circumstances. I suppose some people in my life expected that from me.

Being the eldest American-born daughter of a Native American-Mexican mother while growing up in the United States, I have always been surrounded by a rich tapestry of cultures that shaped my identity in profound ways. My mother, who carried the wisdom of her Native American ancestors and the vibrancy of Mexican traditions, filled our home with stories, rituals, and values emphasizing deep connections to the earth, spirituality, and family. Despite not having a father present in my early years, knowing that I also carried Puerto Rican and French heritage on his side, my mother insisted that familiarizing myself with my father's heritage was just as important as my Native American-Mexican and American cultures.

My mother was a migrant worker, moving from farm to farm with four children in tow, doing her best to provide for us even though she didn't speak English. It took her a decade to get her green card and several more years to become a United States citizen. There were countless hardships, moments of uncertainty, and many times when I felt the weight of being the oldest.

While I could recount childhood traumas dating back to those early years, significantly shaping my outlook, self-esteem, and cynicism, I will spare you the details. Instead, I emphasize that while those experiences influenced my perspective, they do not define me. They are parts of my story, fragments of experiences that built my subconscious mind.

What defines me is the resilience I learned from my mother, the ability to embrace my multifaceted heritage, and the strength to rise above the challenges, especially when being told I did not belong, hearing the constant, "Wet-back, go back to where you came from!"

My journey, shaped by these cultural complexities and difficult circumstances, is one of survival and self-discovery and has led me to understand that I am more than the hardships I've endured. I am the culmination of strength, heritage, and hope.

My dreams defined my high school and college experiences, more challenges, and an unwavering belief in a successful future; whatever it looked like, I knew it would be amazing. As a freshman at West Leyden High School in Illinois, I had an ambitious goal: to graduate early and head straight to college, bypassing my senior year. Although it wasn't a typical path then, I was determined to make it happen. I believed in my ability to succeed, no matter the obstacles. What can I say? I have always been a dreamer.

Back then, I was resolute in carving my path. I tackled a rigorous course load, balancing academics and extracurricular activities like chorus, dance, soccer, basketball, theater, and the French club, all while working part-time at Portillo's Beefs and Hotdogs. I was driven by the idea of an early graduation and eager to move on to the next chapter of my life.

One day during my first year of high school, I went to the guidance counselor's office to discuss my plan. What started as a conversation about credit requirements and summer school options quickly took a surprising turn. The counselor's response was disheartening: "Well, I suppose girls like you need to graduate early to help your family." Her assumption that a Mexican girl like me wouldn't pursue college but would instead focus on supporting her family was incredibly biased.

It was like my balloon full of bright hopes was suddenly punctured by a sharp pin. Instead of discussing college prospects or scholarships, I was dismissed and stereotyped. However, rather than letting this discourage me, it reignited a fire within me. I worked tirelessly, graduated high school as a junior, and immediately enrolled in the local community college. Although I couldn't graduate on stage with my peers, I counted it as a success.

At Triton College, I dreamt of becoming a world-renowned architect, envisioning a future filled with global adventures. Navigating the scholarship program was challenging without parental guidance or school support, but I remained hopeful and determined. However, after a few semesters, I encountered significant challenges, especially with subjects like algebra and calculus.

Later, I discovered I have dyslexia, which explains why I struggled more than my peers. Seeking help, I approached a college counselor, hoping for guidance. Instead, I was again met with discouraging remarks: "You're in over your head! Architecture isn't suitable for someone like you. Men tend to thrive in architecture, women not so much."

Disheartened, I was removed from the architecture program and placed into a general studies designation. It was a huge blow!

I never lost hope despite paying for classes out of pocket and struggling without scholarships or grants. I dreamed of getting my Ph.D. and a vivid image of my mother at my graduation, her heart swollen with pride as I received my diploma. Although that vision has yet to materialize, my journey took a different path. I transitioned to criminal justice, attended the police academy, and pursued a career in law enforcement. While I didn't achieve a college degree, I earned certificates that, at the time, were good enough.

When I decided to pursue a career in law enforcement, it came as a surprise to my family. At that time, I was searching for fulfillment. I temporarily paused my college education due to a lack of financial support, marriage, and raising two young children.

I worked as a facilities manager at a local recreation center, a role I thoroughly enjoyed. I managed the facility, scheduled the front attendants, was a Spanish teacher to elementary school children after school, and was a soccer coach. Work was fun, although the pay was meager.

During that time, I regularly interacted with local police officers, which led to their persistent suggestions that I should consider joining the force. Despite my reluctance, one officer handed me an application for a reserve officer position. He explained that I would only need to commit 30 hours a month, and the department would sponsor my attendance at the academy, conveniently held at my local community college, where I could earn college credits.

My bilingual ability in Spanish was an asset, as the department needed more female officers and had no officers fluent in Spanish. I would check both boxes. This encounter marked a turning point in my life, and I will always be grateful for the officer's encouragement and belief in my potential.

I was persuaded to give it a try, after all, what did I have to lose? With that, I embarked on my law enforcement career. After two years, I moved to Florida and continued my journey in law enforcement. I secured a job with the police department before moving, which was a huge help. It was there that I genuinely excelled and found my calling. Throughout my years in this field, I encountered both thrilling and challenging moments, but I wouldn't trade any of those experiences for anything in the world.

Today, I am the Founder and CEO of two distinguished companies: Women in Protection LLC and Progressive Investigations Research and Consulting Corp (PIRCC). Women in Protection is a pioneering security firm specializing in the training and deployment of women for executive protection roles and providing comprehensive, executive-level security consulting services. Our mission is to provide exceptional, discreet security solutions while empowering women in the traditionally male-dominated executive protection field. Additionally, we offer specialized international child custody support services, assisting families facing the profound anxiety and complexity of recovering children abducted to countries outside the United States. Through both ventures, I am committed to delivering excellence, innovation, and compassionate service to our clients.

Throughout these experiences, my belief in my abilities remained steadfast. Each setback and discouraging word only strengthened my resolve. I knew I was capable of greatness and refused to let anyone define my potential. This chapter of my life is a testament to the power of determination, hope, and an unwavering belief in oneself.

THE LEARNINGS

Life presents us with defining moments, instances that test our resolve, challenge our identity, and push us to crumble or rise. Though often painful or difficult, these moments become the crucibles in which our character is forged.

One such moment occurred during my high school years. A teacher who was supposed to nurture and encourage young minds told me in front of the entire class that I would never amount to anything. Her words cut deep, leaving me feeling humiliated and small.

But rather than let her words define me, I used them as motivation to prove that I am someone and that I, too, deserve the opportunity to shine. Despite her opinion of me, I was so determined that I also signed up for her class the following year. I didn't just want to prove I could do it; I wanted to prove to myself that I was better than that.

Each obstacle, each doubt cast upon me, became a stepping-stone towards my ultimate goal. I worked tirelessly, often late into the night, driven by the desire to succeed not just for myself but for every person who had ever been told they couldn't.

When I went into law enforcement, I had challenges not just from my male colleagues but also from women. One woman said, "You know you were only hired because you speak Spanish." Honestly, I was okay with that. To me, that meant I had a skill she didn't.

Men often asked me why I wanted to be a police officer; I could get hurt, they'd say, hinting at the fact that I was a woman and may not be capable of protecting myself. You would think that would no longer be the mindset. However, I can tell you I still see this attitude toward women in my profession. I never let those comments hurt me or stifle my determination. I dealt with these and many challenges on my own.

In Florida, I worked for the Clearwater Police Department and the Pasco Sheriff's Office. I was surrounded by people and an entire department that made it clear how they felt about Mexicans. Anytime we had a special assignment with a federal agency, I would hear, "Hey, Rodriguez you're getting deported!" or "The white vans are here, Rodriguez, hide." I was the only Mexican in the department and the only one fluent in Spanish. At some point, I realized they needed me. With this understanding, I would grin at the comments and didn't allow it to get under my skin.

During the early stages of my career in law enforcement, I had the opportunity to serve in various roles. These included being a hostage negotiator on the SWAT team, and the Crisis Management Team. I also had the privilege of working as an undercover narcotics detective, instructing defensive tactics, teaching driving skills to police department personnel, and dedicating myself to investigating human trafficking cases, among other responsibilities.

Each role brought unique challenges and opportunities, shaping my career in ways I had never imagined. The most amazing part of my job was the sense of fulfillment I felt at the end of each day, knowing that I had done something good for someone. That feeling became my driving force, my "drug." It was what I craved, the knowledge that I had made a difference. I focused on making someone smile, whether a child, a prisoner, or a colleague. This sense of purpose and fulfillment became the cornerstone of my career in law enforcement.

One of the most important lessons I've learned is the power of resilience in the face of adversity. Throughout my journey, I have encountered people and situations that tried to define me by their doubts, biases, and limitations. However, I turned those challenges into stepping stones rather than accepting their judgment. My experiences have shown me that it's not the words of others that shape us but how we respond to them. Every setback and negative comment fueled my determination to prove to myself that I was capable of far more than they ever imagined. This resilience became my foundation for growth, and each victory, no matter how small, reaffirmed my belief that I could carve my path, no matter the odds.

When we stay true to ourselves and our purpose, we tap into a power that can break any barrier.

I've also come to realize the importance of self-belief. Even when others dismiss your capabilities or try to diminish your worth, believing in yourself is the greatest tool for success. It's easy to internalize the negativity around us, but true strength lies in rejecting those external judgments and focusing on our inner voice. When we stay true to ourselves and our purpose, we tap into a power that can break any barrier. My story is about overcoming hardship, embracing that inner strength, and using it to inspire others, especially women in male-dominated fields, to pursue their dreams and assert their value. We each have a voice, and we can create meaningful change through that voice, supported by our actions.

THE INSPIRATION

My mother has been my most significant source of inspiration, especially during the toughest times. Her unwavering strength and resilience in the face of adversity have profoundly shaped who I am today. Watching her navigate challenges with grace and determination taught me the true meaning of perseverance. No matter what obstacles came her way, she always found a way to move forward, never allowing hardships to define or hold her back.

Her selflessness and dedication to our family constantly reminded us of the power of love and commitment. She instilled in me the belief that anything is possible with patience and hard work. Even in moments of doubt or difficulty, my mother's quiet courage and unshakeable faith served as a beacon of hope and motivation.

Whenever I felt overwhelmed by life's challenges, I would draw strength from her example, knowing that if she could overcome her struggles with four children, surely, I could too. Her influence continues to guide me, reminding me that resilience, compassion, and unwavering determination are the keys to overcoming adversity.

My passion has been shaped by role models, literature, and personal experiences, each contributing uniquely to my outlook on life. Princess Diana stands out as a significant role model for me. Her resilience and ability to face challenges with grace and compassion have influenced my approach to adversity. Watching her navigate her public and private struggles with dignity inspired me to remain strong and composed, no matter the circumstances.

In literature, the works of Edgar Allan Poe and Native American folktales have profoundly impacted my understanding of courage and resourcefulness. Poe's exploration of the human psyche and the darker aspects of life taught me the importance of facing my fears. At the same time, Native American stories emphasized the value of wisdom, bravery, and adapting to one's environment. These tales instilled in me a deep appreciation for the strength that comes from within and the importance of using one's inner resources to overcome obstacles.

My inspiration has certainly evolved throughout my journey. As I've grown older, the relationships I've developed with colleagues and others have become significant sources of inspiration and, at other times, some hard lessons. These connections have offered new perspectives and reinforced the importance of collaboration and mutual support in personal and professional settings. The shared experiences and wisdom from these relationships have guided me, helping me navigate the complexities of life and career with greater understanding and resilience. The more difficult relationships have strengthened me, much like the wounds on our skin; when it heals, the skin is visibly tougher. It is the same with the wounds caused by relationships that didn't last. However, these difficult relationships also provide an opportunity to learn a lesson. You might even learn something about yourself. It provides an opportunity not to blame others, however bad they may be to you, but to search from within and dig deep to correct old programming that may no longer serve you, for example.

Another profound shift in my inspiration has been the deepening of my reliance on faith and spirituality. Over time, spirituality has become a cornerstone of my life, providing a sense of peace and balance that I previously didn't fully appreciate. As I progressed in my career and faced the inevitable growth challenges, my faith offered a steady foundation, helping me stay grounded and focused on what truly matters. This blend of strengthened relationships, spiritual growth, and career progression has reshaped me into a better person.

I now draw motivation from external achievements and an inner sense of peace and purpose, allowing me to approach life with a balanced perspective and a deeper understanding of what brings lasting fulfillment.

THE ADVICE

Looking back, offering advice to my younger self would center on patience, self-compassion, and embracing the journey rather than obsessing over the destination. In my youth, chasing immediate success and validation was easy, leading to frustration when things didn't unfold as planned.

I would remind my younger self that growth is gradual and that every setback or challenge is an opportunity to learn. It's okay not to have everything figured out right away, and the pressure to meet expectations shouldn't overshadow the importance of well-being and happiness.

One significant mindset shift I wish I had embraced earlier is that failure isn't something to fear but a crucial part of learning. When I was younger, I often saw failure as a reflection of inadequacy, which fueled self-doubt. Over time, I've learned that failure is a stepping stone to greater success.

> *Failure isn't something to fear but a crucial part of learning.*

Mistakes provide valuable insights, build resilience, and ultimately lead to achieving goals. I would encourage my younger self to take more risks and view every experience as a valuable lesson.

Another piece of advice is to use your voice. I hesitated to speak up for myself for a long time, unsure if it was okay or how to do it. If I had known what I do now, I would have spoken up much sooner. Learning to assert myself has been critical in building confidence and earning respect. It's important to understand that your voice matters and that it's okay to use it to advocate for yourself, your beliefs, and others.

To someone on a similar journey, I'd advise trusting the process and being patient with yourself. Life rarely unfolds in a straight line, and there will be moments of uncertainty and difficulty. These moments are part of the journey and make you stronger and wiser.

Maintaining a sense of balance is also crucial. It's easy to get lost in pursuing career goals or personal ambitions, but nurturing relationships, caring for your health, and finding time for joy are equally important. This ties into the concept that you can't pour from an empty cup. You must first take care of yourself before fully giving to others. If you're constantly running on empty, you won't have the energy, focus, or emotional reserves to support others or pursue your goals effectively. Taking time to recharge and tend to your needs is necessary for sustained success.

Several habits have been instrumental in my growth.

First is mindfulness. Practicing mindfulness has kept me grounded and present, especially during stressful times. It has helped me manage emotions, stay focused, and maintain inner peace despite external turbulence. Mindfulness fosters self-awareness, enabling me to recognize and change unhelpful thought patterns.

Regular reflection is another crucial habit. Reflecting on experiences, decisions, and emotions has deepened my self-understanding. It has allowed me to identify areas for improvement, recognize patterns that held me back, and celebrate progress. Reflection is also a powerful tool for setting goals aligned with my values and making choices that support long-term growth.

Cultivating a strong support network has also been instrumental. Surrounding myself with positive, like-minded individuals has encouraged me during tough times, offered new perspectives, and held me accountable. I've learned the importance of seeking out mentors, friends, and colleagues who inspire and challenge me to be my best self.

Embracing a growth mindset has been crucial to my development. Believing that abilities can be developed through effort has empowered me to approach challenges with curiosity rather than fear. It has allowed me to see obstacles as growth opportunities and persevere in adversity.

Finally, I would advise my younger self, and anyone on a similar journey to be patient, embrace failure as a teacher, use your voice confidently, and maintain balance.

Remember, you can't pour from an empty cup, taking care of yourself is essential for personal and professional success. Mindfulness, reflection, a strong support network, and a growth mindset have been crucial to my growth, helping me navigate challenges and stay true to my values.

THE PATH FORWARD

The legacy I hope to inspire in you through my story is one of resilience, self-compassion, and the courage to use your voice. I want people to see that it's okay to face challenges and setbacks, they are not failures but stepping stones to growth and success. My journey is a testament to the power of perseverance, the importance of maintaining balance, and the significance of taking care of oneself along the way. Too often, we hold back, fearing judgment or failure, but in doing so, we miss out on the opportunity to make a difference in our own lives and the lives of others.

By sharing my experiences, I hope to encourage others to embrace these paths, with all the twists and turns that come with them, and to understand that the process of becoming who you are meant to be is just as important as the destination. It's crucial to remember that personal growth is a continuous journey, not a race, and that evolving at your own pace is okay.

Listen closely to your inner voice, thoughts, and words; they carry your truth. As I began to reflect on my life, I noticed a remarkable pattern: the things I spoke or thought often came to pass. Sometimes, my intentions manifested almost instantly, yet others unfolded years later. But they always materialized. I've come to understand that when our words and thoughts are aligned with intention, they hold immense power. Be mindful of the intention behind your words, for they often reflect what you truly believe, that is your reality.

My call to action is to be brave enough to take risks, embrace failures as learning opportunities, and prioritize your well-being as you chase your dreams. Again, you cannot pour from an empty cup; taking care of yourself isn't just about self-preservation; it's about ensuring you have the strength and energy to make the impact you are meant to make.

If you got this far and reading this stirs something within you, a desire to make radical changes, then it's time to believe wholeheartedly that what you want is possible and already within reach.

Any doubt will throw your dreams off balance. So, believe it deeply, feel it in your bones, write it down, say it out loud, and make it happen.

Your life is yours, and you must embrace the change with confidence and intention.

I want you to know that you are enough, your journey matters, and you have the power to shape your legacy. By embracing your own story with authenticity and courage, you can inspire others to do the same.

That, I believe, is the most powerful legacy of all.

ABOUT MONICA

Monica is an esteemed security leader with decades of corporate security, protective services, investigations, and law enforcement expertise. Her extensive experience designing and implementing security plans minimizes liability risks while effectively safeguarding valuable assets globally in various sectors. With fluency in English, Spanish, intermediate French, and Italian, Monica excels in communicating and adapting to diverse environments. During these war times, Monica has served as a go-to resource for employees and high-value assets strategic extraction from areas such as Lebanon and Israel.

Monica has excelled in various roles throughout her illustrious career, showcasing her exceptional skills and dedication. She has served on the Human Trafficking Task Force, worked as an Undercover Narcotics Detective, and utilized her negotiation expertise as a SWAT Hostage Negotiator. You can read more about all of these in her new book, "Vast Potential: A Bodyguard's Journey to Empowerment," which will be published in March 2025.

Monica's professional journey has taken her across the globe, providing executive protection and staffing for ultra-high-net-worth families in international settings and delivering services on multiple continents. Monica's passion for mentoring and sharing her expertise is evident through her involvement in publications and hosting a weekly show on Women in Protection. She takes pride in guiding professionals, helping them unlock their potential and excel in the security industry. Monica's exceptional character and ethical conduct set high standards for others to follow, earning her respect and admiration from her peers. Monica has been featured in the New York Times and The Daily Mail, she has also been published and quoted in multiple security books, and articles in industry publications.

For more information, visit Monica Duperon Rodriguez's official website: http://www.monicaduperon.com

> *Surround yourself with Extraordinary Latinas who encourage you to thrive.*

UNITED LATINAS

ABOUT UNITED LATINAS

Elevating the Voices, Leadership, and Impact of Extraordinary Latina Leaders.

UNITED LATINAS is a collaborative organization devoted to empowering, amplifying, and connecting Latina Women to elevate their leadership impact and presence by providing upskilling workshops, public speaking programs, mentoring, leadership development opportunities, visibility, networking, and community-building platforms and programs.

At UNITED LATINAS we know that finding community and building professional alliances can be a powerful source of growth and inspiration. That's why we strive to create a space where Latinas from around the globe can come together and find commonality, support, and encouragement.

At UNITED LATINAS, we believe that Latinas deserve to be seen and heard. We work to amplify the voices of our community, increase their visibility, and expand their leadership presence and impact. Whether you're a seasoned leader or just starting out, we offer a variety of development programs, visibility platforms, and resources to help you upskill and grow.

Ready to take the next step in your leadership journey? Join us and discover the power of connecting with other like-minded Latinas!

www.unitedlatinas.com
hello@unitedlatinas.com

UNITED LATINAS Mighty Hub
Your Gateway to a Powerful UL Online Experience
https://unitedlatinas.mn.co

ABOUT THE PUBLISHING AUTHORS

ILHIANA ROJAS SALDANA

ILHIANA ROJAS SALDANA is a Human Potential & Culture Expert, an Award-Winning Advancing Women & Hispanics Advocate, an Executive and Leadership Coach, a DEIB Consultant, a seasoned multicultural Business Strategist, a Bestselling Publishing Author, and an International Motivational Speaker.

Ilhiana has over 20 years of global executive experience in top Fortune 500 companies in Mexico and US headquarters, leading and coaching professionals, teams, and businesses into success. As the founder of her first company BeLIVE Coaching and Consulting, Ilhiana is a certified expert in leadership and DEIB best practices that help build resilient, collaborative, and high-performing leaders and cultures. Ilhiana has mentored and coached leaders of all levels and has delivered impactful coaching programs to over 3500 professionals across multiple industries and sectors worldwide.

Her strong commitment to advocating for equity led her to co-launch a second company UNITED LATINAS Corp, leading as Co-President. UNITED LATINAS is a women's empowerment and leadership development organization providing upskilling workshops, mentoring opportunities, leadership and professional development programs, visibility, networking, and community-building platforms and programs. She has also been the driving force in the launch of four women's leadership development programs in Europe, LAM, and the US to reduce the gender gap, and has been the publishing author of two Best-selling Anthology books, sharing the stories of 30 Latina leaders.

Before starting her two companies, Ilhiana was a highly respected global business leader and seasoned strategist with extensive multicultural experience driving transformational change through deep consumer understanding, developing breakthrough business strategies, and building high-performing and engaging cultures. She has played key leadership roles in companies including P&G, Hanesbrands, and Hasbro, acquiring a strong understanding of consumers of all ages, genders, ethnic and cultural backgrounds. During this time, Ilhiana drove double-digit growth across numerous businesses and returned a business to profitability after years of net losses, and earned several recognitions and awards for her strategy, innovation, and positive team culture.

In addition to coaching, Ilhiana is actively involved in different diversity, equity & inclusion initiatives with a focus on empowering women and the Hispanic population in the corporate and non-profit sectors. She has served as Chief Development Officer for ALPFA (Association of Latino Professionals for America) Boston Chapter, and a Founding Board Member for Thousand Faces and GetWise. She also serves as an advisor for the Rhode Island Hispanic Chamber of Commerce, the Center for Women & Enterprise (CWE), Social Enterprise Greenhouse (SEG), and several other private organizations and institutions. Furthermore, she is an Executive MBA Career Advisor for the Hult International Business School.

Ilhiana's most notable awards and recognitions include the 2024 Most Influential Woman Powerlist by COLOR, 2024 Top 100 Latinas by Latino Leaders, 2023 P&G Alumni D&I Award, the 2023 Top Coaches Award by WomELLE, and the 2022 Women in Business Stevie Gold Award among others.

Ilhiana graduated with honors as a Chemical Engineer in Mexico City, and lives in Rhode Island with her family.

Learn more and connect with Ilhiana at:

www.belivecoach.com
www.ilhianarojas.com
https://www.linkedin.com/in/ilhiana-rojas7
ilhiana@unitedlatinas.com

SANDRA NOEMI TORRES

Sandra Noemi Torres is a visionary leader, accomplished business strategist, and impactful speaker dedicated to driving transformation and empowering individuals and organizations to unlock their fullest potential. With over two decades of expertise in marketing, sales, and business development, Sandra has built a distinguished career helping brands expand their reach, increase market share, and craft compelling narratives that resonate on a global scale.

As the founder of SNCO and a trailblazing force in the marketing and advertising industry, Sandra has worked with top executives and businesses to create high-impact strategies and advertising campaigns. Her ability to identify untapped opportunities and drive innovative solutions has positioned her as a trusted advisor to leaders seeking exponential growth.

Sandra's passion for supporting and amplifying Latinas led her to start an organization to provide training and leadership development. In 2018 she founded UNITED LATINAS to create a platform for Latinas to come together, learn from one another and gain new skills to advance their careers, businesses and lives. Sandra is the CEO for UNITED LATINAS, a thriving women's personal development organization that empowers Latina women. She spearheaded the creation of Latina Speakers Club, a leading Latina Speakers Training and Development program and the Latina Speakers Directory where Hispanic women are showcased and highlighted for visibility. Her commitment to fostering meaningful change has earned her recognition as a catalyst for empowerment, bridging opportunities for underrepresented communities and being recognized as a Hispanic Women of Distinction in 2024.

Recognized for her thought leadership and impact, and honored for her contributions to business and community development. Sandra also serves on multiple boards and provides coaching, consulting, and mentorship to CEOs and their organizational team.

Beyond her professional achievements, Sandra is a lifelong learner with a deep fascination for the intersection of human potential, neuroscience and holistic well-being. Whether through her dynamic workshops, compelling thought leadership, or transformative consulting, she inspires others to embrace their unique journey, break barriers, and achieve unparalleled success.

Sandra is a Serial Entrepreneur also owning an ecommerce brand, House of Gnostic and a coaching and consulting practice that supports entrepreneurs and individuals looking to launch a business.

Sandra is a multiple time published author with her book The Life Agreement, The Speaking Effect, The Goal Getter's Diary and a collaborative project & #1 Amazon Best Seller, Extraordinary Latinas Vol II - Breaking The Narrative & Redefining Our Power.

Learn more and connect with Sandra at:

www.SandraNoemi.com
www.PlanYourCompany.com
www.HouseofGnostic.com
www.linkedin.com/in/sandratorres
Sandra@UnitedLatinas.com
www.UnitedLatinas.com